Indian Novelist of the Contemporary English Literature

Dr.M. Ananthi Devaraj

Published by

BONFRING®
Intellectual Integrity

Indian Novelist of the Contemporary English Literature

9 789386 176110 >

ISBN 978-93-86176-11-0

Author

Dr.M. Ananthi Devaraj

Bonfring

309, 2nd Floor, 5th Street Extension, Gandhipuram,

Coimbatore-641 012.

Tamilnadu, India.

E-mail: info@bonfring.org

Website: www.bonfring.org

Phone: 0422-3928700

Dedicated to

My Family

Preface

Indian English Literature has attained an independent status in the realm of world Literature. Wide ranges of themes are deal with in Indian Writing in English. While this literature continues to reflect Indian culture, tradition, social values and even Indian history through the depiction of life in India and Indians living elsewhere, recent Indian English fiction has been trying to give expression to the Indian experience of the modern predicaments. There are critics and commentators in England and America who appreciate Indian English novels.

English has acquired a rare privilege and popularity in India especially among the elite and the middle classes. It is increasingly being used by writers to give shape to the conflicting dilemmas and issues that confront the human psyche. It has definitely become a convenient medium to express the intrinsic talents of the writers. Moreover the Indian English writers use it with enviable ease and gaining mastery of a foreign tongue to articulate the vagaries and vicissitudes of an individual's consciousness in a realm of its own aptly substantiate the expansiveness and verve of the Indian English writer.

Indian writing in English has commended unstinted admiration in both home and abroad and, is now in its full swing. It has carved out a new track, a new vision-a vision that is replete with an unanswering faith and hope, myths and traditions, customs and rites etc. A deep dive into the works of the Indian stalwarts of English fictions, reveals that their works are not an imitation of English literary pattern but highly original and intensely Indian in both theme and spirit.

They have given a new shape and color to English literature in the same way as the Australians and Americans have evolved their own literature in their respective countries.

Indian English literature is two hundred years old. Sri Aurobindo's works stands like a huge oak spreading its branches over these two centuries. The contribution of Sri Aurobindo as a perfect writer and craftsman is undoubtedly great. He is the first poet in Indian English writing who has given the re-interpretation of myths. Sri Aurobindo envisages spiritual humanism.

What Sri Aurobindo points out to the philosophers of today is that human life, body and mind are the evolved forms of super mind. Aurobindo's famous works *The Human Cycle* and *The Ideal of Human Society* taken together to give a complete picture of Aurobindo's version of the future possibilities of man and shows the humanistic trend in his thought. In *the Human cycle*, the poet–philosopher offers us a social philosophy of history illuminated by a splendid spiritual vision of future.

Rabindranath Tagore (1861-1941) is a celebrated name in the sphere of English literature. His creative genius is so much accounting and his literary output is so much rich and varied that the phrase 'myriad - minded', which Matthew Arnold had used for Shakespeare, can aptly be used for him also. He won the Nobel Prize for literature in 1913, for his immortal poetic work *Gitanjali* (1913).

Besides being a great universal poet, the genius Tagore is also a novelist, dramatist, Short-Story writer, musician, philosopher, painter, educationalist, reformer and critic in every field and had earned a niche for himself. The setting of his novel is representative and reflective; the characters are natural, realistic, full -blooded and life -like.

The socio-religious culture of Bengal is brilliantly portrayed in his novels. Through his novels he brings out some of the problems of the woman of his age. Different kinds of human relations are portrayed and analysed through the different social settings. Some of his novels deal with the modern problems of our society and the interest in them centers round the psychological development of characters under the compelling stress of circumstances. To his credit, there is a long list of poems and plays, both in Bengali and English which had made his place among the world's greatest writers.

Indian English literary personalities like Rabindranath Tagore (*Sadhana*) or R K Narayan (*Malgudi days*), later novelists like Kamala Markandaya (*Nectar in a Sieve, Some Inner Fury, A Silence of Desire, Two Virgins),* Manohar Malgaonkar (*Distant Drum, Combat of Shadows, The Princes, A Bend in the Ganges and The Devil's Wind*), Anita Desai (*Clear Light of Day, The Accompanist, Fire on the Mountain, Games at Twilight*) and Nayantara Sehgal have ceaselessly captured the spirit of an independent India struggling to break away from the British and traditional Indian cultures and establish a distinct identity.

Indian English Literature pertains to that body of work of writers from India, who pen strictly in the English language and whose native or co-native language could be one of the numerous regional and indigenous language of India. English literature in India is also intimately linked with the works of associates of the Indian diaspora, especially with people like Salman Rushdie who was born in India but presently resides elsewhere.

During the 1980's and 90's, India had emerged as a major literary nation. Salman Rushdie's *Midnight's Children* had become a rage around the world, even winning the Booker Prize. The worldwide success of Vikram Seth, *Midnight's Children* made him the first writer of the Indian Diaspora to enter the sphere of elite international writers and left an indelible mark on the global literary scene. Other Indian English literature novelists of repute of the contemporary times include-V.S. Naipaul, Shobha De (*Selective Memory*), G.V. Desani, M. Ananthanarayanan, Arun Joshi, Khushwant Singh, O.V.VIjayan, Allan Sealy (*The Trotternama*), Sashi Tharoor (*Show Business, The Great Indian Novel*), Amitav Ghosh(*Circle of Reason, Shadow Lines*) and others.

The writer in the genre of Indian English literature, who took the world with a storm, was Arundhati Roy, who's *The God of small Things* won the 1997 Booker Prize and became an international best-seller overnight. Rohinton Mistry, Firdaus Kanga, Kiran Desai (*Strange Happenings in the Guava Orchard*), Sudhir Kakar (The *Ascetic of Desire*), Ardeshir Vakil (*Beach Boy*) and Jhumpa Lahiri (*Interpreter of Maladies*) are some other renowned writers of Indian origin.

The mid-twentieth century Indian literature in English had witnessed the emergence of poets such Nissim Ezekiel (*The Unfurnished Man*), P Lal, A. K. Ramanujan (*The Striders, Relations , Second Sight, Selected Poems*), Dom Moraes (*A Beginning*), Keki N. Daruwall, Geive Patel were profoundly influenced by literary movements taking place in the West, like Symbolism, Surrealism, Existentialism, Absudism and Confessional Poetry. These authors heavily had made use of Indian phrases alongside English words and had tried to reproduce a blend of the Indian and the Western cultures.

Indian English literature is an honest enterprise to demonstrate the ever rare gems of Indian writing in English. From being a singular and exceptional, rather gradual native flare-up of geniuses, Indian English has turned out to be a new form of Indian culture and voice in which India converses regularly. While Indian authors–poets, novelists, essayists, dramatists–have been making momentous and considerable contributions to world literature since the pre- Independence era, the past few years have witnessed a gigantic prospering and thriving of Indian English writing in the global market.

Not only are the works of Indian authors writing in English surging on the best-seller list, they are also incurring and earning an immense amount of critical acclamation. Commencing from Mulk Raj Anand, R.K.Narayan, Anita Desai, Sarojini Naidu, Toru Dutt to Salman Rushdie, Vikram Seth, Allan Sealy, Amitav Ghosh, Jhumpa Lahiri, Chitra Banerjee, Arundhati Roy, Vikram Chandra the panache of fine Indian writers is long and much augmented.

1. DEPICTION OF WOMEN CHARACTERS IN THE WRITING OF SHASHI DESHPANDE

Shashi Deshpande occupies a significant place among the contemporary women novelists who concern themselves with the problems of women and their quest for identity. Shashi Deshpande is an award winning Indian Novelist. She published her first collection, of short stories in 1978, and her first novel. *The Dark Holds No Terrors* in 1980.

Shashi Deshpande is a winner of the Sahitya Academy Award, for the novel *That Long Silence.* Her works also includes children's books. Shashi Deshpande's novels present a social world of many complex relationships. In her novels many men and women living together, journing across life in their difference age groups, classes and gendered roles.

Shashi Deshpande's Novels deal with the women belonging to Indian middle class. She deals with the inner world of the Indian women in her novels. She portrays her heroines in a realistic manner. As *The Dark Holds No Terrors,* the novel reveals the life of Sarita, who is always neglected and ignored in favour of her brother; she is not given any importance.

In 'Root and Shadows' explores the innerself of Indu, who symbolizes the new women, who are educated and married to Jayant but her feminine instinct for articulation is suppressed and Mini inculcates in her all the traditional feminine qualities since her childhood. Akka got married to a man who has much older than her. She has to tolerate the scathing and bestial sexual advances of her husband.

In the novel *That Long Silence* Shashi Deshpande reveals that Consciousness of Jaya through an exposition of her mind in the process of thinking, feeling and reacting to the stimuli of the moment and situation.

Jaya is not totally a silent and mute sufferer. Her stories are filled with compassion and understanding for the characters, especially the women.

Her stories explore the search of a woman to remain as a human being in spite of playing her role as a daughter, wife and mother. Her stories show the anguish and conflict of the woman caught between patriarchy and tradition on one hand and her self-expression, individuality and independence on the other hand and the transition she undergoes.

Shashi Deshpande's focus is on women. But the difference lies in the way she looks at them as human beings and not as mere women and also writes about the various problems they face, both at personal and societal level. Deshpande's gallery of women consists of mothers, daughters, sister-in-laws, mother-in-laws, co-sisters, wives, single women, widows, women deserted by husbands and so on.

Dealing with women of different age groups ranging from a fourteen year old girl to a sixty year old lady; and different types of women like single, married, divorcee, widows and spinsters her stories explain the problems and dilemmas in their lives.

Her women characters have strength of their own; in spite of their challenges and hostilities they remain uncrushed. She does not portray all the women characters in the same mould. Just as two people do not react in the same way to the same situation in real life, no two of her women characters react in the same way to the same situation.

If some are revolting, some are placid. Some seem to be mature and some are in transition.

Mostly, she presents her women characters as persons in the journey of self-realization.

In *The Dark Hold no Terrors*, Saru is the heroine. The novel is the story of a marriage on the rocks, Sarita called Saru is a "two in one woman", who in the day time is a successful doctor and at night a terrified trapped animal in the hands of her husband, Manohar. He is a English teacher in a third rate college, is a jealous husband and is the victim of inferiority complex. Saru is not happy in his company and is unable to fear the sexual sadism of her and her problems ensue because of her outsized ego and innate love for power over other.

Saru defies traditional code at the slightest threat to her importance as that in what she missed and craved for in her mother's house. She is a broad minded woman and realizes that economic independence alone could be an insurance against subordination or suppression. Her husband is not an ordinary male chauvinist. He is very much shocked when an interviewer asks him that How does it feel when his wife earns not only the butter bus most of the bread as well?.

It undermines his confidence totally. He lets his wounded male pride sexual sadism. Saru's brother Dhruva, unfortunately dies by drowning into the water and her mother makes her feel quality of his death. That fills revolt in her against her mother. She is a courageous woman and does not care for the harsh words of her mother.

Through her Character the novelist wants to project the post modern dilemma of a woman who strongly resents the onslaught on her individuality and identity. The antagonism is faced mainly from two person Saru's mother and Manohar, saru's husband.

Both of them represent the values and norm established by the patriarchal society. She wants to be a strong woman in all the three angels, biological, psychological and social in the end of the novel.

She identifies herself with the roles fulfilled. She decides to cut off the traditional bonds of marriage and home and walks into the wide world. It is her comprehensive realization of "self" in which the consideration of family society and personal relationship assume a pigmy position.

In the novel *That Long Silence*, the narrative is fabricated at two levels: one represents the inner world of Jay's consciousness reflecting her discontent of personal life and on the other, Shashi Deshpande reflects on the various dimensions of problems of women in the traditional society of India. Mohan, the husband of Jaya is an engineer by profession; Mohan's cencerm is basically with the externals such as money, status, material comforts.

Jaya is a very bold lady. Jaya's father taught her to have confidence in herself and has taught her lessons of morality Jaya is not one merely a housewife but she is also a career woman. She is successful columnist and an aspiring writer of fiction. She writes serous stories and sends them to magazines. But her husband is a materialist man and has no craze for her creative genius. Apparently Jaya adjusts with it but gradually if becomes a burden to her.

Her marriage is loveless which causes the wife and the husband to drift away from each other. She is ever hunted by the memories of the past, her earlier life and her marriage with Mohan. In the end of the novel she decides to put an end to her long silence. She recollects the triumph with the present with which her father had named her Jaya, 'Jaya for victory.' She is renamed as Suhasini. Now she is soft, smiling, placid motherly woman.

She tries to remove her long silence and struggle with the problems of self revolution and self estimation.

Jaya has decided to come out form her house to the open word and decides to show her talents. She reminds the words of Kamat which he said her long away that "pursuit of happiness is meaningless and loneliness is the essential condition of human existence". Everyone has to fight his own battle. The novel becomes a self critique of Jaya. She has fathomed the darkness of herself and learnt to articulate her predicament. Thus in her novels she has given the outer and the inner self of her all male and female.

In the novel *Roots and Shadows* the author gives a clear picture of the prevailing problems of a joint family. At the outset the family seems to be whole and unique but the subtleties inside the family that have been portrayed, by the author exhibit the reality of a joint Indian family. The author has made one point very clear that the head of a family should be more tough and steady to run a family.

To keep order and harmony in a family, it needs an indomitable spirit; one must evaluate the pros and cons and make decisions for a family, because one is responsible for solving the problems as well as maintaining peace in the family. In this novel such a character is AKKA, who is endowed with authority and domination.

Indu was basically rebellious in nature. She left her home for study in the big city when she was a teenager. She aspired to be a journalist and became what she dreamt of. She fell in love with a young man who seemed to be modern and married him. In due course, she realized that her freedom was illusionary. She has exchanged the orthodoxy of the village home for the conventions of the 'Smart young set' of the city where material well-being had to be assured by sacrificing principles, if necessary.

Through her novel, she expresses the frustrations and disappointments of women who experience social and cultural oppression in the society.

Women build harmonious relationship in a spirit of give-and-take and in a mood of compromise and understanding. They undergo the process of transformation and change their perspective to cope with life that remains the same. They do not change the situation but change their outlook. This is the common thread found in many of her short stories.

2. SELF-EXPLORATION IN SHASHI DESHPANDE'S THAT LONG SILENCE

God shaped the world with wonderful creations, but God's most beautiful creation is women. But their life is not created beautiful. It is full of agony. They have to struggle to overcome the problems till their end. A Woman is protected by her parents at her girlhood, after the marriage, she is looked after by her husband. At the old age, she was used to spend remaining years of her life under the roof of her children without any will or desire and rights in the family. In brief, she had no personality of her own. The agony of a woman is portrayed in the character of Jaya in Shashi Deshpande's novel *That Long Silence.*

Among Indians women English novelists Shashi Deshpande occupies a prominent position. She wrote ten novels, six collections of short stories, four books for children. Shashi Deshpande is an award winning Indian Novelist. She is the second daughter of famous Kannada dramatist and writer shriranga. She was born in 1938 in Karnataka and educated in Bombay and Bangalore. She published her first collection, of short stories in 1978. She is a winner of the Sahitya Akademi Award, for the novel *That Long Silence.*

Jaya is a modern woman rooted in tradition, whereas her husband, Mohan, is a traditionalist rooted in customs. The difference between their outlooks is so great that they fail, repeatedly, to understand each other. To Mohan, woman sitting before the fire, waiting for her husband to come home and eat hot food is the real strength of a woman, but Jaya interprets it as nothing more than despair. The difference in their attitude is the main cause of their failure to understand each other.

Due to differences in attitude, their marital life grows unsteady and gloomy. It becomes more of a compromise than love, based on social fear rather than on mutual need of each other. The cause may be rooted in their choice of a partner. For example, from the very beginning, Mohan wanted a wife who was well educated and cultured and never a loving one. He made up his mind to get married to Jaya when he saw her speaking fluently, sounding so much like a girl whom he had seen speaking English fluently. He tells Jaya:

> You know, Jaya, the first day I met you at your Kamukaku's house, you were talking to your brother, Dinkar, and somehow you sounded so much like that girl. I think it was at that moment that I decided I would marry you. (90)

Mohan, the husband of Jaya has least concern for the family. But he poses himself or believes that he is the one ideal husband. He wants to give his children what he did not get as a child. He is clear about himself. "he was a dutiful son, he is a dutiful father, husband, brother"(9). Jaya gets irritated when he says, "It was for you and the children that I did this. I wanted you to have a good life. I wanted the children to have all those things I never had."(9).

In this novel, right from the beginning Jaya maintains silence; and finally she breaks her silence in order to step forward to lay claim for a prosperous life. How it happens is what the novel is about. Jaya, the protagonist of the novel *That long Silence*, like every other Indian woman within the patriarchal system, suppresses her own likes and dislikes, as she plays second fiddle to her husband during crucial times, in her own words "I had learnt it at last no questions no retorts, only silence". (143)

Jaya's husband, Mohan was that sort of a man and he married her for his social betterment. Jaya had lost her father at the age of fifteen and her brother considered her a burden and this lead her to marry Mohan. Before her marriage, Jaya had been taught the importance of the husband in the life of a woman. Vanitamami tells her that a husband is a sheltering tree.

Ramukaka reminds her of the thing that the bliss of her husband and home depends entirely on her. When Jaya is leaving her home after her marriage, Dada has advised her to be good to Mohan. Jaya's brother brought Mohan with money and gave him to Jaya and she tried to be good to him. This was the beginning of Jaya's lifeless kind of married life.

The entire novel brings out the stale married life in a middle class home and Deshpande tells the story from the point of view of a wife. The women in Mohan's family were so definite about their roles and duties. But Jaya has no clear cut idea about her role in that family. Concerned only about the tastes and interests of Mohan, Jaya has lost her realism as a human being. She has shaped herself to the wishes of Mohan.

Mohan kept her away from her likings. She was forced by Mohan to given up the job she wanted to take, the baby she wanted to adopt and the anti-price campaign she had wanted to take part in. Jaya's journey through the rough road of her nuptial life, she learns at last: "no questions, no retorts: only silence".

Since Jaya got married, she has done nothing but wait. Waiting for Mohan to come home, waiting for children to be born, for them to start school, waiting for them to come home, waiting for the milk, the servant, the lunch carrier man...(30) This mechanical process of waiting fills her life with existential nothingness.

Her monotonous, boring and isolated days made her to realize. The entire novel bring out the stale married life in a middle class home. The married life of Jaya seems to have lost its freshness.

As a typical Deshpande's heroine, Jaya does not decide to walk away from marriage or think about a divorce. Instead she has decided to tackle her marital problems in her own way, and make her husband realize that she has to be treated on an equal footing, without destroying the status of her family life. Mohan had left home without a word after Jaya uncontrollably laughed at him. His absence unnerves Jaya and she thinks, she would fall apart.

Jaya is forced by events beyond her control to seek refuge at her first home, after marriage. Husband Mohan, has been accused of stealing of office funds and, on the advice of some friends, is in hiding for some time. Jaya was not supported to Mohan's business malpractices in the company. Away from her children and alone with her husband, Jaya understands dearly many aspects of her life and relationships that she had avoided or failed to realize earlier. Her decision to write as she wishes to is rendered possible only after this home coming.

Jaya needs a period of physical and mental withdrawal before she is able to come to terms with her expectations of life. When Mohan walks out of the Dadar flat, she is in a state of turmoil. Alone at home, with only Mukta and Nanda to nurse her back to normalcy out of her delirium and fever, Jaya is physically alienated from her family-temporarily.

During the next two days she writes, pouring out all that she had attempted to suppress for years together. This writing, during the period of withdrawal, helps her realize that she alone is responsible for both her achievements and failures. She begins to see the truth of the dictum, "do as you desire" only after this period of withdrawal.

The novel ends with a remarkable outlook of Jaya that:

> We don't change overnight. It's possible that we may not change even over long periods of time. But we can always hope. Without that, life would be impossible. And if there is anything I know now it is this: life has always to be made possible. (193)

This concept has a world-wide acceptance. Jaya's expectation for a new life, a better way of living with a better understanding with Mohan is clear in these lines. The most important thing is that it is the ultimate self realization of Jaya. Here Jaya discovers her real problems and finds remedy for that. Deshpande suggests the theme of self realization as a remedy to the suffering of that long silence of women in the middle class educated society than a female domination.

Shashi Deshpande stressed the idea of self realization in all her novels and demands a position for women in the society, without the support of their masculine part. There is no bridge of understanding between the wife and the husband. Though they were living together," but there had been only emptiness between them." This emptiness draws Jaya towards Kamat who is opposite in nature to her husband Mohan.

Though Kamat is not a handsome young boy like Mohan but he is an intelligent man who understands the psychology of woman. Jaya is happy in his company because she can exchange ideas with him. Being an intelligent middle aged man he always appreciated her creative power. Kamat treats her as an equal and therefore Jaya used to feel an ease in his company. She says." I told him thing I'd never been able to speak of not to Dad, not to Mohan." She talks to him about everything, including her parents and his full blooded smile, encourageous her to go on. He encouraged her to write on the issues related with the suffering of woman in society. Jaya is conscious that in gender based social system even basic human sensibility and emotions are classified on the basis of gender assigned roles.

But when Kamat dies she feels heartbroken. Even her corrupt husband has lost his highly paid job and thus she has come to the end of the road. In the moment of crisis, her husband expects her to share his anxiety. He wishes to use his wife as buffer on opiate to soften the impact against himself. But Jaya reacts to the situation differently. She wants to burst out in anger, but she fails to break her silence.

When domination of anger continues for a long time, ego, self crisis reaches its climatic point. Mohan becomes frustrated and leaves the house. Now Jaya was alone she bears him two children and third was aborted. She suffers from isolation. Her marriage is loveless which causes the wife and the husband to drift away from each other. She is ever hunted by the memories of the past, her earlier life and her marriage with Mohan.

In the end of the novel she decides to put an end to her long silence. She recollects the triumph with the present with which her father had named her Jaya, 'Jaya for victory.' She is renamed as Suhasini. Now she is soft, smiling, placid motherly woman. She tries to remove her long silence and struggle with the problems of self revolution and self estimation. She has decided to come out from her house to the open word and decides to show her talents. She reminds the words of Kamat which he said her long away that pursuit of happiness is meaningless and loneliness is the crucial condition of human existence. Everyone has to fight his own battle. The novel becomes a self realization of Jaya. She understands the darkness of herself and learnt to evaluate herself.

3. Social Realism in Mulk Raj Anand's Untouchable

Mulk Raj Anand, a socially committed novelist, has produced a good deal of literature. He has written more than a dozen novels and about seventy short stories and a host of essays and articles on a number of subjects. His novels fall into two categories namely social and autobiographical novels. He focused his attention on the sufferings, misery and wretchedness of the poor as a result of the exploitation of the downtrodden class of the Indian society.

Religious hypocrisy, feudal system, East-West encounter, the place of woman in the society, superstitions, poverty, hunger and exploitation are his common themes. His famous novels namely *Untouchable* (1935), *Coolie* (1936), *Two Leaves and a Bud* (1937), *The Sword and the Sickle* (1942) *and The Road* (1963), which deal with poverty, hunger and exploitation as their major themes.

Untouchable is a sociological novel which seeks to stress the evils of untouchability by focusing attention on the miserable plight, suffering, poverty and degradation of a large section of Indian Society. Bakha as an untouchable seeks his freedom in the infallibility of caste discrimination, with its hypocrisy, cruelty, deceit and inhumanity. He stands passive and bewildered at the immensity of horror hoping for a change. Bakha, thus, is a symbolic figure, a universal figure, who stands for a large segment of Indian Society which had been doomed to suffering since times immemorial.

The novel covers the span from 1930 to 1940 when poverty, slavery and the inhuman exploitation of the masses were at the peak. It was Gandhi who had waged a war against the forces behind these evils. The novel describes a single day in the life of the protagonist Bakha, a scavenger boy.

The entire action takes place within a period of less than twenty four hours. Though the scene of the novel belongs to a small, interior town of the Punjab, the happenings are pan Indian in character. Bulandshehar, a small town with an outcaste colony on the outskirts represents a normal Indian town found anywhere in India.

Bakha is a young boy of eighteen who has not surrendered to his fate like his father Lakha. He is a child of twentieth century and is given to modern way of dressing. He dreams of a good life but as soon as morning dawns his job of toilette-cleaning starts. Three rows of latrines to clean single handed, and several times too; to bring cleanliness in the place of filth and possible disease; such is Bakha's daily toil which he turns into a dexterous art.

In all the incidents that took place in the novel *Untouchable* including: Temple Incident, Bazar Incident, Hockey Match Incident, Well Incident-the hero has to suffer due to the curse of untouchability, so vehemently criticized by M.K. Gandhi. The water problem among the untouchables is depicted through the 'Well Incident.' They were not allowed to touch even the brook or pond, as they would contaminate the stream. They had to wait hours beside the well and had to request the upper castes to pour water in their pitchers. They weren't allowed to 'touch anything that touchables touched'. This is the cruelest irony of life that even for water, the basic necessity of human existence, the sweepers has to depend on the mercy of the caste Hindus.

During his psychological transition from innocence to experience, he faces identity crisis. Initially he possesses no awareness of being an outcaste. The kind treatment from the White Tommies makes him feel superior to his fellow outcastes and this superiority complex is reflected in his attitude and appearance.

He does not live unclean or uncouth like other scavengers. His intelligence, sensitivity and the air of dignity differentiate him from his fellow outcastes.

Even a high caste Charat Singh feels "Here was a low caste man who seemed clean" (23). He calls Bakha a gentleman. But his role as a gentleman is thwarted by a series of incidents that happen during a single day. He suffers without any fault of his own. The slap he receives from the high caste Brahmin for defiling him by his touch makes him aware of his true identity. Soon after this he faces another moment of humiliation at the steps of the temple that increases the rage in his soul. But the molestation of his sister by the priest turns him violent to which he reacts aggressively.

The giant stride of the sweeper towards the temple frightens the crowd. "His fist was clenched. His eyes flared wild and red, and his teeth ground between them the challenge: 'I could show you what that Brahmin dog has done!'"(86).

But his hereditary serfdom acts as a handicap to his spontaneous rebellion. He realizes that he can do no more than being enraged against the brutalities of the high castes.

Instead of appreciation, Bakha receives condemnation even when he saves the child from an accident and takes him to his home lifting on his hands. The thankless mother of the child shouts at him for defiling her house and wounding her son. He thus receives inhuman treatment from almost everybody. They throw things at him the way they do to the animals.

This inhumanity reaches its climax when a so called mother throws a thin slice of bread at him from the top of her house. He feels ashamed of himself for picking up the bread from the pavement.

Bakha wants to protest but he who cleans the filth of the people becomes aware of the filth around him. He realizes that he is surrounded by his own people who are meek, humble and who have accepted exploitation as their fate. His father tries to calm him down by making him realize that such exploitation is not unknown to their caste. His sister, Sohini, also tries to pacify him by asking him to accept it as a part of their destiny. His inability to revolt should be perceived as an outcome of the oppression of the outcastes for thousands of years.

His submission to the superiors who exploit him is the result of the inborn slavery that he inherits. Bakha imitates the life style of the Whites and desires to live life in their manner. While copying the White sahib in all regards, his excessive 'fashun' makes him an object of ridicule. Some of the critics call it a colonial exploitation of Indians by the British.

It is important to discover whether Bakha's imitation of Tommies is a symbolic representation of the youth in Pre-Independent India or an untouchable's natural reaction against the exploitation by the high caste Hindus. If it is considered as a symbolic representation of the youth, such a reaction was generally found in the rich and educated high caste people and not in the downtrodden outcastes. It must be a reaction to the treatment he receives from the high caste people.

Though he has a number of characteristics of a hero, he cannot revolt openly against exploitation as a modern hero does. He belongs to the transitional period. His father Lakha symbolizes the servile attitude of the last generation who cannot even think about the revolt. The feeling of revolt grows in Bakha's consciousness due to the bitter experiences he has. However this urge to revolt could never be materialized as it was practically not possible for an outcaste to revolt against the higher classes.

This passivity or helplessness of Bakha is a true reflection of social reality in the then India.

Bakha's father Lakha is the symbol of passive submission to the exploitation by the high castes. He represents the force of tradition, orthodoxy and conservation. He does not blame the high caste for the exploitation but blames himself for this fate. He believes that his birth in the low caste is the result of their sins committed by him in the previous birth. He does not get angry even when Bakha tells him about the molestation of his daughter. He cannot even think about revolt against the stubborn order. He is so afraid of them all that when Bakha talks about retaliation, he says,

> "We cannot do that. They are our superiors. One word
>
> of theirs is sufficient against all that we might say before
>
> the police. They are our masters. We must respect them
>
> and do as they tell us. Some of them are kind."(109)

Bakha's thought of retaliation against the established system becomes significant when we compare it with the passive submission of Lakha to it. Pundit Kali Nath is the priest of the temple in the town. This so called custodian of Hindu religion and culture turns out an ill humoured devil.

Though he is a priest he lacks the real strength of a spiritual person. His moral weakness is exposed when he tries to seduce a sweeper girl. When he fails in his sexual assault he accuses her for defiling him. Through the character of Kali Nath, Anand brings out the underlying hypocrisy of the high caste advocates of the so called morality and culture. It has been a custom in most of the villages of India to convert the low caste girls into 'Devdasis'. The girls are married to the god but are used by the priests to satisfy their sex hunger.

Those who firmly believe that the touch of the outcaste defile them, do not get defiled when they sleep with the untouchable women.

Anand shows his concern over the organized evil in the society which is the cause of the miseries of the outcaste downtrodden. This organized evil is the real enemy of the society. It deliberately denies the basic human rights to the unprivileged class. Caste system kills the human dignity by giving an unfair advantage to a certain class over the others on the basis of their birth which damages the homogeneity of the society.

Anand wants to awaken the exploited, suppressed, dehumanized classes of the society. He feels that exploiting the proletariat has been our national sin which we have been committing for centuries together. They are forced to such a depth that they will sink lower and lower and cannot rise above. They have been pushed to such a lowly life that it makes them feel subhuman. Anand wants to uplift them from the deeps. Bakha endures his social exploitation for quite a long time in the novel.

As a realistic novelist, Anand does not end the novel with the happy union of the two classes. He knows that untouchability is deeply rooted in the Indian psyche. The high caste youth 'Sanju' accepts the compromise to work with untouchables only superficially. He returns to his people and shows his arrogance, which is his true nature. He kicks the brass cup of water from Bhikhu's hand and mourns. "Our whole house will have to be purified"(110). The attitude of all the friends of Sanju clearly shows that the youth of the high caste Hindus is not ready to accept the change

Considering the reflection of reality in the novel, it can be observed that the characters and events in this novel are related to the persons alive and the events occurred in early twenties in one of the provinces of India. The major incident is based on Jawaharlal Nehru's *An Autobiography* (1936) which Anand has reviewed such as Kissan's march towards Allahabad to make the politicians aware of the inhuman treatment to the peasants by the landlord and Nehru's approval to visit the place to make an enquiry form the core of the plot. The arrest of Lalu and his comrades and their trial are historically true. The period at the background of the novel is a transition period in the history of India both politically and socially.

4. Multicultural Literature in the Novel of Arundhati Roy

Literature in English is a global phenomenon. It has become usual that literature in English always emerge all over the World, thus literature in English is becoming increasingly multicultural. The International writers use English as a channel for poetry, fiction and other genres. Thus literature in English has become multicultural concept since the global writers have been writing about given culture.

In the present global scenario, English literature commands the realm of multicultural literature. Sir Walter Scott, one of the multicultural writers wrote about Scotland for English readers as well as for his fellow citizens.

Multicultural literature explicitly reflects the works of multicultural societies and also it is implicitly multicultural.

Multiculturalism has become a reality now. No nation can exist without a multicultural existence. No race, no religion, no caste, no tribe, no language can claim to be superior to others. As particles of an atom are different, fingers of a hand are different, brothers and sisters of a family are different, and variety is the very essence of creation, whether it is human beings, other beings, or inanimate objects. It is selfish to call a place-village, town, city, district, state or country-as one group's and deny others entrance to it.

During the last fifteen years, multicultural texts were found in the writings of R.K. Narayan's *The Painter of Signs*, Maxine Hong Kingston's *The Woman Warrior,* Rudolfo Anaya's *Bless Me, Ultima* and Witi Ihimaera's *Tangi.* Though these texts have been received well, certain critics do not compromise with the multicultural aspects because of moments of difficulty in four such multicultural narratives.

The multiculturalism of contemporary world literature in English poses complex problems that have not been sorted out by critics who studied the multicultural phenomenon. It is observed that all the written texts of multicultural literature were not completely understood by the readers of same language. Such texts are fully explicit. Such problem frequently occurs between the speakers of same language.

Indian constitution has played a vital role in promoting the value of multiculturalism, which brings the people of diverse religions, culture and backgrounds together. The social aspects of multiculturalism are depicted in the Indian English fiction. It tries to show that all members of society, regardless of their caste and religion, have equal opportunity to reach their full potential with dignity and respect.

Arundhati Roy is the author of the novel, *God of Small Things*, which received the prestigious Booker Prize in 1997. Arundhati Roy's maiden novel, *God of Small Things* claimed immense critical acclaim from readers and critics throughout the world. The novel received praise for various aspects like the shifting of past and present with extraordinary finesse, her flair for description and its narrative style which includes magic, mystery and sadness.

Arundhati Roy's *The God of Small Things* Roy's protest in *The God of Small Things* spring out from her sense of the slave like status of women in free democratic India. The marginalization of women is not a specific but a global phenomenon. It differs according to regions. Arundhati Roy offers a kind of direction to change the status of women in the Indian society. So the novel is not only a story of Ipe family, but also of the disempowered section of Indian society. Arundhati Roy's first book The God of Small Things was an immediate success. More than 350,000 copies were sold within the first three months after publication. It has been distributed in thirty countries and translated into twenty-four languages (Tikkanen). The reactions to this novel were mostly positive throughout the world. Nevertheless, in India it received widespread criticism. One of the main criticisms was its topic.

The policies of multiculturalism have been violated to some extent. Multiculturalism is a very flexible theory that promotes cultural coexistence and mutual respect to all communities and castes irrespective of their differences and distinctiveness. Irrespective of culture, subculture, caste and community, every individual has his/her own birthright to enjoy his/her free life. Life is a gift that everyone gets by God. So respecting of each other's culture is respecting of each individual.

By handling the theme of inter caste love affair, Roy tries to highlight the need of a casteless and peaceful society where everybody's interest should be protected and respected for strengthen of the principle of democratic multiculturalism. Disrespect of any culture, creates social unrest. Sometimes the multicultural policy in India gets disturb due to misunderstanding of caste stigma and social structure based on class culture and religion.

Although it is so it is our duty as conscious individual and citizens of India to respect the Indian constitution and the principle of multiculturalism. So that everyone could get a space to stand with each other with equal dignity and to breathe the free air in the real multicultural country like India.

The novel narrates is the tragic story of Velutha, the protagonist, whose life is ultimately destroyed by the combined forces of religion, tradition and society. Apart from Velutha's tragedy the novel focuses on the anguished world of Esther and Rahel, the twins, who become the part of this tragedy. Arundhati Roy adopts a narrative which is satiric in tone and lashes her anger on the rigid age old caste system which dominates our society.

The novel talks, among other things, about politics, religion and caste, topics that people normally do not talk about. The second major criticism was her description of the love between Velutha and Ammu. Roy was accused of obscenity and faced a trial in India. It is quite interesting that even though the affair between Velutha and Ammu were not the only scene that talked about illegal love (there is also child abuse and incest), these scenes infuriated the public most. It was probably not so much because of sex, but because Velutha was from a lower caste than Ammu (Tikkanen).

The God of Small Things talks about the history of a ruined middle-class family. The book starts with the introduction of the first incident that started a chain of tragic events: the funeral of Sophie Mol, the cousin of the main heroes Estha (Esthappen) and Rahel. They were fraternal twins of a divorced mother, Ammu, who after leaving her husband came to live with her parents and her brother Chacko. The book provides its readers with many examples of the local customs, religion, political scene, the oppression of women and the difficulties connected to the caste system.

The most active character is Velutha, an Untouchable worker in the family's pickle factory. He belongs to the lowest caste, which means that his life is full of restrictions and without possibilities of advancement. The Kochamma family admires his skills, yet he is still subordinate to them.

Velutha tries to break the laws: he has a better job than is suitable for his caste and he is a member of the Communist Party as well. These are small things for ordinary people, but not for an Untouchable.

The first part of the book contains many descriptions and sidetracks and the story evolves slowly, introducing the characters, the settings, the past and the present. Suddenly, the story starts to gain speed and the events follow in short succession. As the narrator puts it: things can change in a day.

Sophie Mol joins the twins during an attempt to run away from home, but she drowns in the river. Velutha's father tells Ammu's mother, Mammachi, about their children's relationship, consequently Velutha has to hide. His hiding coincides with Sophie Mol's death and he is accused of killing her and kidnapping the twins.

The twins and Velutha hide in the same house, where the police beat him almost to death. Mammachi forces Estha to lie that Velutha kidnapped them. Estha makes the false accusation at the police station, but never speaks again. Velutha dies in prison, Ammu hasto leave Ayemenem sending Estha to his father and leaving Rahel with the family. The book ends as it started with the meeting of the estranged twins Estha and Rahel trying to find their way back to each other.

5. IDENTITY-CONFLICT IN ARUN JOSHI'S THE FOREIGNER

Arun Joshi is one of the most prominent writers among the Indian English novelists. He grabbed the attention of readers as well as critics by his new thematic concerns in the genre of novel. Arun Joshi is a novelist who, more strongly than most, has brought to his work that detachment from the everyday, while still acknowledging its existence, which is perhaps India's particular gift to the literature of the world.

Arun Joshi's first novel *The Foreigner* was first published in the year 1968. Arun Joshi has candidly accepted, with reference to The Foreigner that his recurrent theme is alienation which is closely related to the identity issues in many forms, sometime in the form of identity conflict, sometime in the form of self-quest, many times leading to estrangement from the self. At the same time, his heroes are intensely self-centered persons, prone to self-pity and escapism.

In all his novels, Arun Joshi attempts to deal with different facets of alienation, in relation to the self, the society around and humanity at large. Sindi Oberoi in *The Foreigner* (1968) is a born Foreigner-a man alienated from all humanity like Mahatma Buddha, he spent his life in search of the self and the identity of himself, leading to-Enlightenment at Nirvana (Death of the life). The process of developing self-identity has three stages. The issue of identity-crisis and self in the novels of Arun Joshi is the result of philosophical (Buddhist school of thought), psychological output of personality traits and sociological Cultural shock. The Foreigner relates how Sindi Oberoi, an immigrant Indian, suffers in the course of his search for meaning and purpose of his life. Sindi's alienation from the world is similar to the one that many existentialist heroes in the west suffer from.

The novel is an enactment of the crisis of the present in the story of Sindi Oberoi. The question is of the identity as self-identity of a person who does not know his birth, parents, relatives and friends. This very understanding of Sindi brings Joshi closer to Camus and Sindi to Camus'outsider.

Sindi was himself an emotionally sterile person devoid of the self and the identity. It seems that Sindi was selfish and his philosophy of detachment was merely a false construction to run away from the worldly responsibility towards June. It is not that Sindi could not start a fresh life with a meaning and self identity but the precedent experiences were obstacles to do so.

The climax of the novel comes at a juncture where June, deprived of love and marriage by Sindi, falls in love with Babu Rao Khemka and it is aptly reciprocated by Khemka. Sindi was in past deep love with June and he could have saved the life of both Khemka and June but now he is guilty of killing the duo. Sindi has committed a crime because of his false detachment. A man without identity, roots, values, ethics, emotions and love cannot be expected to be redeemed.

Arun Joshi by his own inventions and discoveries makes Sindi to realises. After coming to India, Sindi got a God-sent opportunity to redeem himself. Muthu and his problems bring about a major change in Sindi's attitude towards life. The Indian soil gives him a meaning to life, attachment from self to the world. In The Foreigner, Arun Joshi depicts a keen awareness and deeper understanding of our times. Sindi represents the solutions to the meaninglessness of life.

The establishment of the identity of Sindi at the closing of the novel presents the only way of saving man from the purposelessness and degradation of the contemporary meaningless world. At times, the identity of Sindi could be compared to that of Karna of Mahabharata because both the characters suffer from the identity conflict and crisis, but at many times the resemblance is quite contradictory as well.

The identity-conflict in the protagonist of *The Foreigner* is many-folded. Though Sindi involves himself in an earnest quest for life-sustaining values, he is not able to overcome the miseries of past completely. The character of Sindi portrays the sense of metaphysical anguish at the meaninglessness of life. Lastly, what comes out from the conflicting nature of the protagonist of The Foreigner Sindi Oberoi, is that life rotates in a flashback style. The identity conflict in The Foreigner in the light of the character of Sindi reveals that man's false beliefs and self-created agenda of life evaporate with the passage of time.

The identity of Sindi is not only the identity of a character of Arun Joshi's *The Foreigner*, it is also an identity of the millions of the young generation of the world, who have a lot of questions but no answer. The identity of Sindi is a warning to evolve a system to meet the needs and challenges of the time. What Sindi did was the outcome of the social conditions. That Sindi loves but cannot marry reflects the identity-conflict and he is torn apart between West and East.

Arun Joshi's fictional world is most strange. One of the most significant contemporary Indian novelists writing in English, Arun Joshi has focused not on social or political problems but on the deeper layers of man's being. The very core of the thesis Conflict in Arun Joshi's Novel is not one-sided; rather it is multi-dimensional and multi-faceted, encompassing philosophy, psychology and sociology.

It seems to distil the essence of the dilemmas and quests of Arun Joshi's protagonists conflict. The conflict that erupts in the protagonists of Arun Joshi's novel has the form of craziness, pain, agony, the selfishness of love, the mystic realities of life in a gentle tale, centering on the various aspects of life, bringing out the vitality of life, normal and the abnormal, the ordinary and the extraordinary, illusion and reality, resignation and desire, etc.

The conflicts between alienated self and the socio-cultural forces are the postulates of Arun Joshi's fictional creations. In all the novels, the protagonists of his novels are subjected to extreme social, cultural and psychological pressures. This search of the identity is the central pillar of Arun Joshi's novels. The alienations that emerge in the novels of Arun Joshi are because of the clash between the socio-cultural and psychological pressures. The alienation arises because of the social maladjustment and emotional insecurity; this alienated self leads to a psychological revolt within the self that every moment of life is in search of identity.

Arun Joshi has, in *The Foreigner*, very dexterously handled some-thought provoking, grave issues like, rootlessness, detachment, frustration, quest for better alternative, identity-crisis and self-realization, highlighting India's glorious cultural heritage and imperishable moral values.

6. ALIENATION IN ARUN JOSHI'S THE STRANGE CASE OF BILLY BISWAS

Arun Joshi represents a consciousness that has emerged from the confrontation between tradition and modernity. In analyzing Arun Joshi's ideas, one finds that his experience is based on vision of life. He minutely observes the conflict between the traditional values and the modern materialistic approach to life. With his deep knowledge of Indian philosophy, he suggests in his novels an entirely Indian solution to the spiritual crises of the youth.

The Strange Case of Billy Biswas is seemingly a sequel developed from the first novel The Foreigner. Sindi and Billy Biswas, the protagonists of *The Foreigner* and *The Strange Case of Billy Biswas* respectively, seem to explore the hidden treasures of life; they search for their own bearings of life and death, sorrow and joy. Their major concern is their real and the inner world -the world of soul. This very communication is also the beginning of the establishment of self-identity, if not the assertion of the identity. Here was the entering into a new world –the world of the supernatural.

In the novel *The Strange Case of Billy Biswas*, Arun Joshi portrays how the process of individualization destroys a man of extraordinary sensibilities. The novel seems to advocate that life's meaning does not lie in the world outside but within.

The quest for identity of Billy Biswas is deeper than that of Sindi Oberoi of The Foreigner. Arun Joshi in this novel has tried to combine the Lawrentian quest for the essence of life with Upanishadic search for soul's spiritual reality.

In reality, Billy learns from the seers, mystics and visionaries of all ages and it brings him closer to Mathew Arnold's Scholar Gipsy, as a result of which Billy takes the hard decision to live in the jungles of Central India deliberately renouncing the luxurious life that he could have afforded very well. Billy is completely faded up with the grossly materialistic Indian society, in defiance of its traditional values, ethics, culture and mores. It also endorses that Billy supports the anti-materialistic way of Hindu life.

Romi, his room partner at the Harlem in America, opines that Billy was the man of extraordinary intellectual man of extra obsession. But what even he fails to understand was his real identity and thus the question still persists with Billy-Who am I? Billy's case is a strange case because of the fact that his personality was split between modernity and primitivism. This opinion of Billy makes him understand that he was not meant and made for this world and that is why this society was misfit for him.

In reality, the first section of the novel is a background to understand the psychologically tortured Billy Biswas that how he was in constant conflict and in his quest of identity. The life he was supposed to live was miles away from the life of tribal in reality. The elite culture-laden society did fit to the quest of identity for Billy and he returns to India. But, to his utter surprise, he finds Delhi not different from the American society and feels Delhi's high hybrid society to be spiritually deserted and emotionally alienated.

Billy hates the worldly pleasures but Meena is fond of the money, market and the materialism, supposedly the identity of the elite society. Arun Joshi successfully represents here that his protagonist was not an abnormal person.

Rather he was very much a part of the human society and had the wish and desire to give a new identity and meaning to life by establishing a family.

But, at the same time he portrays that Billy is destined by his very nature for some other person and places. It brings the character of Billy closer to the character of destiny.

The civilized world is unaware of the life of Billy and his whereabouts. Billy has settled in the hills of Maikal with Bilasia as his future and Dhunia, the village headman-as his master. Billy has found the identity of the king and priest in the tribal village, far from the urbanised but dehumanised world. Billy has completely changed. He was found by Romi in the lion cloth typical of the way primitives live in the jungle.

On having a meeting with Romi, Billy narrates his vision of the primitive world and the urge of life for the tribal people and how he has added a new meaning to his life. Billy takes a promise from Romi that he will not disclose the whereabouts of Billy to anyone else. But Romi was not a man to keep his commitments and discloses the whereabouts of Billy to Situ, when forced by Situ to disclose the same.

The disclosure of the whereabouts of Billy to Situ by Romi brings tragedy to the life of Billy. Protagonist Billy has nothing to come back to the city. When Meena and Billy's father come to know about the reappearances of Billy they start a hunt for him. They do not realize the case of Billy and insist on meeting him without his consent. In the village, none tells the whereabouts of Billy. It shows the respect and love the village people have for to Billy.

Meanwhile a rumour spreads that Billy has killed a constable and then the atrocious torture of the state machinery operates in the jungle and ultimately Billy is killed. On his tragic death, Billy, Billy remarks: You Bastard. The bastard symbolises the hatred of Billy for the civilised people of the urbanised society.

The quest for identity was the prime motive of Mr. Billy Biswas. The whole novel is devoted to the search of identity. Billy from his childhood was filled with inquisitiveness.

7. MARITAL DISHARMONY IN ANITA DESAI WHERE SHALL WE GO THIS SUMMER?

Anita Desai is specially noted for her sensitive portrayal of the inner life of the female characters. Several of Desai's novels explore tensions among family members and the alienation of middle-class women. She explores the intricate facts of human experience bearing upon the central experience of psychic tensions of characters. Her chief concern is human relationship.

Her central theme is the existential predicament of an individual which she projects through incompatible couples–very sensitive wives and ill matched husbands. Desai deals with thoughts, emotions and feelings and not so much with action because she voices the mute miseries and the helplessness of millions of married women through the stream of consciousness technique. She explores the emotional world of women, aware of the deeper forces at work, with a profound understanding of feminine sensibility as well as psychology.

Desai is interested in the motivation and the psychic turmoil of her characters. Throughout the novel *Where Shall We Go This Summer?* Desai makes an attempt to go deeper into the extraordinary inner life of its protagonist, Sita. Part one of the novel deals with the present and immediate past of Sita's life. She, living in her flat, feels bored as members of her family follows their own ways of life. She is a daughter of a political celebrity. As her father was mostly in jail and she has no mother to look after her and she is denied the regular life of a normal child.

Sita lives in the island sometimes alone and sometimes in the company of her brother Jivan with clay and mud. With the passage of time, she finds her father turning an authentic legend on the island and its people respect him for his miracles. After the death of her father, Sita is taken to Bombay by Raman, her husband and the son of her father's old friend Deedar. She leaves Manori with relief, "longing for the same, the routine-ridden mainland as for a rest Sanatorium." (72) Raman later marries her drawn by her beauty.

Eventhough she has four children from him "with pride, pleasure-sensual, emotional, Freudian, every kind of pleasure-with all the placid serenity and supposedly goes with pregnancy and partition." (20) She remains restless and dissatisfied with her settled and dull domestic life.

When she conceives for the fifth time in her forties, she is haunted by a new idea of not giving birth to the child. In order to keep the baby unborn, she desires to take refuge in Manori, the island of miracles. Ultimately she takes her daughter Menaka and younger son Karan with her.

Sita begins to enjoy the peaceful life in the island but Menaka and Karan get bored with it. Menaka sends a message to her father secretly to take them to Bombay for her Medical College admission. Sita does not want to go back and it would be hard for her to make compromises with her husband. She feels betrayed by all and ultimately compromises with the terms of life and accompanies her husband to Bombay.

Sita is a young sensitive and emotional middle aged woman, who has four children. She feels isolated from her husband and her children and becomes the victim of mental agonies because of her psychological contrast between the past and the present.

She thinks of her past childhood, free from all the tension and makes a contrast between her childhood and her present womanhood in which she is thrown to an environment of tension and shadows.

Sita craves to be hugged and loved by Raman. Seeing a couple in the Hanging Garden, loving each other free from all worldly feelings, her heart begins to weep and she utters, "Children only mean anxiety, concern-pessimism. Not happiness. What other woman call happiness is just-just sentimentality." (147)

Sita is unable to bear the violence around her-the quarrels of the servants and the fight amongst the children. She finds it difficult to adjust herself in her husband's family and has longed for the sensitive approach from others. She hates not only the violence around her but violence in the world at large.

Sita is not happy with her indifferent-husband. There is lack of harmony in her life. Like Gautama, Raman also keeps himself busy and indifferent to his wife. She finds her very existence threatened because of her husband's indifference and children growing independent. Raman fails to understand her boredom. This married life presents before her more tensions. This is the reason why she wants to run away from her husband.

Sita is unable to make her existence possible in the ground of patriarchy which binds her to her family. She feels all her life she has submitted her self-reliance and freedom. She possesses an inner fury which makes us think about the problem of life. Desai raises this problem in this novel through Sita.

Sita suffers from father fixation as there is no mother in the offing. But her awareness transforms her and she becomes indecisive as what to do. So she escapes to Manori. Her father fixation ends when she realizes that her father was also responsible for her mother deserting them. Her decision to free herself shows her emerging new image. But Sita's battle with Raman becomes more intense when she becomes pregnant for the fifth time.

Raman scolds Sita's escape to Manori. He feels that a woman's happiness is in the house of her husband. He is shocked when she tells him that the only happy moment in her life was when she saw a man and woman in a very intimate way, in the Hanging Gardens. He feels angry and ashamed of their relationship.

The battle between Sita and Raman is resolved. Sita feels emotionally drained out battling against her husband, her family. She desires to bear the child and returns with Raman to the mainland, signifies her return to life, community and society. Sita tries to achieve harmony in life but against the traditional manner, by her own new way. Her new sense of self-awareness empowers her with an understanding of her position in the family. When she resolves her inner conflicts, she is able to conquer the fear that alienates her from the society.

Desai too very emphatically points to the fact that women make unpleasant compromises for the sake of family. Sita powerfully lashes against Raman her husband. Desai challenges these compromises women have to make for the sake of the powerful patriarchal system.

A common trait in Anita Desai's all major women characters is their longing to be free from all kinds of social and familial involvement. Desai's women characters face a dilemma nurtured by marital disharmony. Desai's achievement lies in exploring the psyche of her characters. She plunges deep into the inner life of Indian women. It is the intimate world of the female self that is revealed in the majority of her novels. But this intimacy does not reject the exterior world.

8. A Critical Appreciation of Vikram Seth's Novels

Vikram Seth is better known as an Indian poet, novelist, travel writer, author, children's writer, biographer and also memoirist. He was born in Calcutta on June 20, 1952 to Justice Leila Seth, the first female High Court Judge in India and Mr. Prem Seth, who was a shoe company executive. He is the eldest of the three siblings. His brother Shantum, conducts Buddhist meditational tours and his sister Aradhana, a film maker, married an Austrian diplomat. Seth's family played an important role in his life.

Seth received his primary education in Dehradun, at the prestigious Doon School from 1961-1967 where many of India's wealthy and well-known personalities have been trained. Seth seems to have "divided feelings about the place: appreciation for the superb education he received, and lingering bitterness towards his classmates" (32), a resentment which came from having being intimidated there. This exclusive boarding school education prepared Seth with the self-assurance and the linguistic gear to health in abroad and it also refined in him a tendency for the mythical civilization of England.

Seth's mastermind was obvious right from his Doon School days. From Doon School, Seth won a scholarship to the Tonbridge School, Kent, England, from where he won another scholarship to Oxford to study English. However he soon diverted to Philosophy, Politics and Economics, partly because his father was a businessman and Seth tried to see things from his point of view. Seth also undertook the study of economics for helping him to view thing sensibly. He took his Undergraduate degree in 1975. It was at Oxford that Seth, gloomily aware of his fondness as a University student, began to mark poetry. Seth condemns these early poems, saying that back then he was extremely skillful. He continued writing poems for his own pleasure. Interestingly, Seth has said that he in fact set up it easier to write because he did not study English literature. Perhaps since he was not made extremely aware of all those literary giants, to whom he has been compared. Then for his postgraduate degree, he left for Stanford University.

Seth staggered upon the translated works of T'ang dynasty Chinese poet Wang Wei. He was so much enthused by these poems that he was unwavering to discover Mandarin so that he would read the original works of the Chinese masters. Seth became adept at thinking brilliance by learning the language so rapidly that within a year he wrote a poem in Mandarin. He had also started writing poetry in English more seriously. Seth was conscious of desirable guidance and so he approached the teachers of the English department at Stanford and secured a mentor in the poet Timothy Steele, who then held a Jones Lecturership in poetry at Standford.

The Golden Gate was written and published in 1986 by Random House. This verse novel won Seth the Common Wealth Poetry Prize in 1986 and at once shot him into the limelight. Apart from its obvious literary merits, the book was a landmark in Seth's career. Seth spent nine months writing *The Golden Gate,* a verse novel of nearly 600 sonnets in iambic tetrameter. "a task which is usually rewarded with charges of lunacy" and for which he of course struggled to find a publisher:

An editor at a plush party
Hosted by Thomas Cook
Where my Tibetan travel book
Was honored-seized my arm:" Dear fellow"
What's your next work?" A novel ..." Great !
We hope that you, dear Mr.Seth"
"In verse , I added. He turned yellow,
How marvelously quaint, " he said
And subsequently cut me dead" (144)

Seth's decision to use an archaic poetical form to write about yuppies and artists living in San Franciso was partly governed by his objections to modern poetry which he felt had become too arcane, too remote from everyday experience. He believed that modern poetry had found because it was no longer accessible to the common reader, a primary preoccupation of Seth's writing.

The Golden Gate reflects its author's keen sense of independence from prevailing literary modes and the desire to recreate in poetry ordinary, everyday situations keeping lyricism to a minimum as well as his distaste for linguistic or formal experimentation. The novel in effect creates a bridge between poetry and the novel form. By using verse as the narrative mode, the novel incorporates not only the linguistic features of poetry but also its formal structures. The narrative rhythm is sustained by rhyme and meter. It is through these two elements that the plot and characters are developed as well.

The Golden Gate is in an in-depth exploration of society specifically American society. With a surgeon's precision Seth examines the fabric of contemporary American society and pinpoints the factors that are tearing it apart.

Critics deride the novel for being hedonistic but on a closer scrutiny it becomes clear that not only does the novel argue against a hedonistic lifestyle.

It also manages to make good sense of the chaos that permeates every stratum of a fast paced culture, ever suggesting remedial measures. The characters in the novel are all young professionals from San Francisco whose love stories and relationships are interconnected by events and meter.

The substance of the novel is firmly grounded in the upwardly mobile 1980s; its characters main concerns are loneliness and the need to find a meaningful relationship. It is a feat worthy of Seth's artistic eclecticism to use "the dusty bread molds of Onegin/in the brave bakery of Reagan."(5.3). Seth's treatment of love and marriage in the novel is strangely reminiscent of the Indian mores which inform *A Suitable Boy* according to which passion is a prelude to disaster. Family, relationships and other non-emotional considerations govern the decisions of one's choice of spouse.

The great achievement of *The Golden Gate* is Seth's ability to fashion a stanza form that is versatile, fast paced, and flexible enough to accommodate the most desperate subject–love, death, friendship, food, wine, music, cats, iguanas scrabble not to mention a no-nukes march, the milieu of San Francisco and *The Golden Gate* itself. In common with *A Suitable Boy,* Seth's novel in verse has sudden variations of pace and switches back lurches of tone from hilarious to serious to sentimental.

Like the later novel, it is also the tale of place as much as a group of people, so much so that Gore Vidal called it the Great Californian novel. Seth was lapped in American and Britains because a novel in verse had not been attempted since Pushkin's Eugene Onegi*n* .D.J. Enright called it "a technical triumph unparalled" and the Newsweek wrote, "an utterly original utterly delightful novel"(Sunday Times, London) wrote:

> A tour de force of rhyme and reasonableness, *The Golden Gate* doesn't only compelling advocate life's pleasures; it stylishly contributes another one to them. (Book Review)

It not only attracted unprecedented attention from all quarters but made its author, the blue eyed boy of recent Indian fiction in English and even placed him in the race for the highest honour, the Nobel Prize. All the national newspaper vied with one another to mark him out as 'a writer with the golden pen', 'a writer with a golden touch', 'a possible genius' and so on.

Seth began work on *A Suitable Boy.* It took six years to write this novel. In the mean time, Seth won another award the Central Sahitya Academy Award (1988) for *The Golden Gate,* and published three more volumes of poetry: *All You Who Sleep Tonight* (1990), *Beastly Tales From Here and There* (1991), and *Three Chinese Poets* (1992).

Seth further displays his capacity for wit in *Beastly Tales from Here And There,* a delightful collection of fables retold in verse with his inimitable charm. There are ten animal fables, two are Seth's original and others are from India. China, Greece and Ukraine. The light-hearted spirit in which it is written speaks volumes for Seth's state of mind at the time he wrote these tales, a time when he was languishing in the heat of merciless summer afternoon, while it was too hot to concentrate on the more substantial *A Suitable Boy.*

Being a retelling of fables, the themes are essentially social and humanitarian but Seth gives them a subtle twist here and there to make the stories co-temporal in their relevance to the ironic of life. In this work Seth pauses to reflect on the changed values of mankind portraying the effect these values have upon one's life. The book is written with verbal levity, but its themes run deep and serious. Seth evinces his superb art in creating a verse form in fables from the traditions of these different countries.

These tales in verse are not merely rhymed doggerels but Structured around the classic tension between good and evil and punctuated by superb illustrations. They appeal as much to children as to adults. This turning of these fables to art constructs as well. Seth does without sacrificing the essential vitality of these tales as stories which express folk wisdom.

The relevance of these folk tales in the contexts of their primary creations and now also comes to his ability to get to certain primal sources of interest in these stories for what they communicate. This often being narration or dramatization of human vice, virtues or sentiments together with a keenly amusing perception of animal behaviour. In their imaginative freedom these symbols come half way from their sources to meet Seth as he gives them a suitable verse form.

Interpretation of beastly behavior is not supplementary to what is human in these poems. It constitutes representation of the complex network of the behavior of man and beast, bird and insect in quasi-human terms. The interest which Seth takes to construct upon such behavior accruing from literature and folklore of the past demonstrates his ability to turn to certain sentiments of more than one tradition in this respect. As to the milieu of his verification in this respect, it can safely be said that he has moved on to greater artfulness in his use of the same.

Thus in constructing Vishnu Sharma's tale out of the *Panchatantra* he does not only create suitable diction for the same, something which brings us to attention with its subtle and direct combination of manners and gestures with available speech as in the cat poems of Eliot or the way Kipling's beasts, fowl and reptile use their voices.

By and large the tales stand as evidence of the law of the jungle, the good guy does not win, though in *The Monkey and the Crocodile* the intended victim outwits the aggressor. Aesop's fable, *The Hare and the Tortoise* is given a very modern twist. The hare plays to the assembled media and becomes a celebrity despite losing the race, while the tortoise fades into obscurity. *The Elephant and The Tragopan*, written by Seth, features all the animals in a forest bonding together to plead with the local human community not to flood their valley.

Writers are of course notorious for writing about themselves while writing about others and these concerns are in evidence in Seth's own poetry. What are of additional interest are Seth's liberalism and the even handiness which permeates all his work and *A Suitable Boy* in particular. He appreciates all three poets equally although their approaches to life are so different from each other, if not mutually exclusive.

Seth's A *Suitable Boy* published in 1993 created literary history with the books mammoth size and the million copies sales. *A Suitable Boy* is a political and social life in India after Independence. Its action climaxes in 1952. It is the year Seth was born in Calcutta. In this novel Seth combined satire and romance to even greater effect that it became one of the most popular topic narratives of the late twentieth century.

The magnum opus *A Suitable Boy* centres on the motif of a young woman's quest for love which in these disillusioned times has become a lost thread. The young heroine of the novel, Lata faces a dilemma over which suitor she should select. The three suitors represent three paths in human life.

The novel is endowed with human appeal. The novelist goes back to the early fifties for artistic effects. It is undeniably threaded with a love and marriage plot but is almost as concerned, intricately so with the economy of village life.

The impact of land reform legislation on cities and villages and the effects of a local currency based on chits. It also focuses movingly and persuasively on the after-shocks of the 1947 India Pakistan partition and the day to day frictions of religious conflict as it happened, the Seth family too being Hindus left Pakistan just before partition. Seth's plot resolutions in *A Suitable Boy* as in his other books, do not always gratify conventional expectations.

In its forbidding size, *A Suitable Boy* has been compared with Leo Tolstoy's *War and Peace* or Marcel Proust's *Remembrance of Things Past* or the Nobel Laurete Naguib Mahfouz's *The Cairo Trilogy.* Seth's technique also brings to one's mind the technique employed by Jane Austen and George Eliot. It is written large with imaginative sympathy and organic sensibility. Though it took him six years to write but his labour has been amply rewarded. The novel has been very favourably reviewed.

The novel won the Connect Award in 1993. Common Wealth Writers Prize in 1994 and W.H.Smith literary prize in 1994 and launched Seth into a slew of interviews, talk shows and book signings on his book tour. Seth says that it took him six years to write and adds and it becomes evident that he is only half joking.

An Equal Music is another romantic novel by Seth minus the satire of *A Suitable Boy.* Seth presents an emotionally rich and brilliantly penned novel set in the world of the European classical music circuit. It is a sensitive story about unrequited love and the struggle between desire and duty, between sound and silence. Central to the story is the reignited love affair of a violinist with a gifted young pianist who is going deaf.

As in *The Golden Gate,* there is still consolation to be found outside oneself in friendship and the natural world. In this novel there is in addition music which transfigures those who play it and which is a sufficient gift. Seth describes the claustrophobic social world of a string quartet, their rehearsals, performances, and the psychology of their relationships with each other.

By turn elegiac and witty, *An Equal Music* introduces the reader to another facet of Seth's unique talent. It marks a breaking away from Seth's earlier self controlled and distanced style of writing. The reason for this becomes clear when Seth reveals that for him music acts as a refuge from the tensions of work and he found it difficult to reconcile himself to the thought of writing about it. Music amounts to a passion, almost an obsession with Seth and this is evident from the style in which *An Equal Music* has been written so different from Seth's previous work, as he strives to capture the essence of music in words.

The characters of *An Equal Music* make the same choice. In a typical Seth motif, musical commotion triumph over physical passion. Unlike his other two works of fiction, *An Equal music* is told in the first person, through the words of Michael. The book is therefore less under Seth's control, the characters assume more importance as Seth is forced to give them certain amount of liberty. The emphasis is on the theme rather than on the story unlike in *The Golden Gate* and *A Suitable Boy.*

Seth's erstwhile levity is lost somewhere on the way. It is not just a coincidence that there is certain darkness in *An Equal Music.* It has a melancholic strain running through it that mirrors a corresponding sadness in Seth's mind. Seth admits this and says that he draws upon his own experience of having been in emotional states like Michaels's.

An Equal Music is thus departure from Seth's earlier work. It represents a sort of coming of age as Seth replaces the partly ironic and humorous treatment he usually accords to love with intensity, almost a compulsion to explore its more serious side. There is no doubt that Seth is quite practical when it comes to love, as is evident from his earlier works where he always seems to tell the reader to take love at its face value and not to give it more importance than it actually deserves. But, in *An Equal Music* Seth's love for music sweeps all reservations aside as he discovers and articulates what it meant to be so passionately in love, whether with a person or with an art form.

Daniel Johnson has praised *An Equal Music* as "the finest novel ever written about music in English" and Maggie Gee wrote "Seth gives the fullest portrait I have ever read in fiction of a musician's relationship to his music."(21)

Vikram Seth has turned his obsessive eye on his uncle and aunt in his latest book. *Two lives* published by Penguin Books India in 2005 is a biography. The book chronicles the lives of two different people who came together at the time of unrest to form an unconventional, although successful partnership. *Two lives* is the first very personal non-fictional work he has ever written.

In *Two Lives* Seth chronicles a couple who married rather late in life but made their marriage endured in spite of all the complexity that surrounded their union. The *Two Lives* of the book belonged to Vikram Seth's great uncle, Shanty Behari Seth and his great aunt Henny Gorda Caro. Seth went to live with them in London, when he was in boarding school at Tonbridge at the age of Seventeen. The curiosity they inspired in him then grew over the years into the kind of obsession that fuels his writing.

Seth says that each of his books has come about because it could not have been unwritten. They announce themselves with urgency to him that he cannot resist. Before his aunt and uncle died, he knew he would have to write about them. He says that there was something in the freedom to examine a life in full that attracted him as well as the intrinsic power of their story.

Seth's uncle was a Hindu from India who went to Berlin to study medicine and settled down in London as a dentist. He had to go through the agony of losing his right arm while fighting the German troops at Monte Cassino, but continued to practice until his retirement. Seth's aunt was a Jew from Germany who escaped in 1939 hounded out by Hilter's genocide to seek safety in England. She had the psychological pressure of leaving behind her mother and sister in hostile Germany. Seth has spent much of the past six years trying to reconstruct their remarkable marriage from letters and memories and interviews he conducted with his uncle before his death.

Seth delineates this decline with great tact and poignancy. One of the implications of his book is how even in most intimate of relationships, each of us withhold a private space. Though Shanti and Henry grew close to each other for a decade, there was a great deal they kept apart. Seth reveals this in reproducing his aunt's letters which hint at a lesbian affair, as well as profound grief at the death of her mother and sister which she was never able to express to her husband. Seth has proved himself to be a suitable digger into the layers of memory with the help of personal conversations, family papers and documented history.

The most striking thing about Seth's oeuvre is its variety as fellow novelist Amit Chaudhuri wrote:

> His career has been one of ceaseless reinvention from
> economist to poet to Travel writer, to novelist in verse
> to popular literary novelist, to librettist, to know what
> next. Skipping from genre to genre, it's as if he's not
> just a writer, but a microcosm of the cultural ethos. (508)

As if that were not enough, Chaudhuri has not mentioned Seth's incarnation as a translator of folk stories and most recently a biographer. Vikram Seth's work is characterized by the innovative recuperation of unfashionable and traditional forms such as the realist roman fleauve and a novel in verse. Such recuperation goes against the current of cross pollination between genres and stylistic experimentation which characterizes other writers like Salman Rushdie or Amitav Ghosh to whom he is often compared.

Reading Seth, one experiences the sense of an old-fashioned conception of the relationship between reader and writer. Engaging the attention and interest of the common reader becomes a programmatic element of both his poetry and his prose and his books reveal a sophisticated yet unselfconscious return to realist narrative and formal poetic structures. A presentation of Seth's work does not easily yield an organic picture, since he has radically changed not only genre but also setting, with nearly every book he has written. These range from India and China to England and the United States. Such diversity makes tracing the evolution of Seth's output difficult and less relevant than it would be to a more homogeneous oeuvre. Nevertheless there are certain threads which run through his work, starting from his collection of poetry.

Similarly, *An Equal Music* despite being technically far from putting off the musically uneducated carries the reader along in general sense, so that one seems to hear the music that one never knew. Even Seth's poetry is not of the kind that is difficult to read and even more difficult to interpret, for he places great emphasis on clarity and on the directness of utterance.

9. Matrimonial Quest is Interwoven in Vikram Seth's *A Suitable Boy*

Marriage is an important social institution in Indian society. Grand Indian weddings are known world-wide. The preparation for such weddings starts from the search of a prospective bride or groom. Vikram Seth beautifully portrays this elaborate process of finding a suitable companion for their children by their parents. The process of search for a suitable boy/girl involves many factors, people, and money and so on.

The novel is the best example of continuation of the tradition of arranged marriage as true to the times of 1950s. In India, marriage is a well-established institution which presupposes certain customs and rites, various values, issues and obstacles. Marriage in India does not merely mean the meeting of two individuals, but it signifies mixing and mingling of two families and involves respecting and understanding the customs and tradition as well as the members of each other's families.

Marriage is an ethnically and socially accepted bond between a man and woman that legitimizes a sexual and economic union. It is seen as a social institution, where the bride and the groom make a commitment to each another. Most of the societies around the world have different systems and limitations concerning wedding which addresses issues such as the suitable age of marriage, rites/rituals to be followed, type and amount of gifts to be given and so on.

In most societies, in accordance these social permit and gendered patterns of living are infused in girls from an early age itself. They are taught to become good wives and mothers. Women, who do not marry, especially in the Eastern nations, are thought to be misfits in society. As many novels deal with human relationships, it is only natural that issues of love, marriage and domesticity become the major themes in many novels. It is interesting to note how different writers in different periods reflect this issue based on their personal and societal experiences.

Vikram Seth's *A Suitable Boy* is structured around pursuit or search. Mrs. Mehra's is in search for a suitable boy for her daughter Lata; Dipankar is in quest for a spiritual base; Mr. Mahesh Kapoor is in quest of a political base and the Nawab is in search of his feudal stability. All these quests are centred in the period of 1951-52. The historical search is interwoven with domestic searches and the novel assumes a socio-political-historical form.

Mrs. Rupa Mehra represents an ordinary mother's character of our society. All mothers have a wonderful dream about their daughter's marriage. They want to bring a suitable partner to their daughters with all the prosperities. The most realized and emotional character is Mrs. Rupa Mehra who has only one mission left in life to arrange a proper marriage for her youngest daughter, Lata.

Mother and daughter are generation apart in their ideas, but not surprisingly they eventually do reach an agreement of sorts, as a result of which they find that they are closer than they had ever imagined. Mrs.Rupa Mehra is a woman who is determined to take care of her family at any cost, in fact, to take care of them even if they do not wish to be taken care of.

Mrs. Rupa Mehra is indeed a remarkable character, and not one is soon forgotten. She is vividly drawn and seems to leap off the page with energy, vitality and wit. Mrs. Rupa Mehra is the typical Indian mother, always concerned about her children and always eager to see to it that they settle well in life. And yet, behind the apparent liveliness and positive tones to the whole mother and daughter drama, there are glimpses of resentment at the limitations of an economic and social world in which women had no future but what their husbands could provide or their fathers, if they had been unlucky in the hunt.

The first statement of the novel itself "You too will marry a boy I choose" (3) becomes the harbinger of all the events that Lata, Seth's female protagonist, is made to experience throughout. Secondly, referring to Savita and Pran, the newlyweds, Mrs. Rupa Mehra states with confidence that "they will be happy" (4) which, in due course, becomes a fact.

Seth, right through the course of the novel, has always portrayed Pran and Savita as an ideal couple. Their love and affection blossom after their marriage. Their mutual understanding and trust towards each other help them in overcoming all the hurdles they face in their life. And Seth makes Lata review her actions regarding her matrimonial situation from the ideal level of Savita and Pran Kapoor's domestic life.

The third statement is again about Lata. Her mother in a moment of annoyance and exasperation think "her younger daughter was going to prove more difficult than her elder" (4). At the moment she does not know how true her forecast is going to be. With Savita she does not have any difficulties, but her problems with Lata are going to be enough to last her a lifetime.

Finally the fourth statement; which Mrs. Rupa Mehra also imparts upon Lata. "What is good enough for your sister is good enough for you" (5). This sage pieced of advice only results in bringing forth a flippant and naughty comment from Lata "We can't both marry Pran." But behind the apparent humorous rejoinder, one could sense a bit of moralizing being done by Seth, almost in the Austen mould. If the beautiful and intelligent Savita is satisfied with the "lanky, dark, gangly and asthmatic"(4) Pran Kapoor, and their arranged marriage, then probably for Lata and for the likes of Lata , that is the ideal state of being, to remain happy and self sufficient.

Mrs. Bennet in *Pride and Prejudice* and Mrs. Rupa Mehra in *A Suitable Boy* are members of the wealthy family and find it difficult to search suitable boys for their daughters. In today's India, this social problem has assumed a monstrous form, where thousands of daughters are burnt for inadequate dowry, where thousands of daughters with scant resources and who are caught in the vicious tentacles of caste, religion and conservative traditions. Vikram Seth, basically an English brown Sahib, sitting away from the growing and unfulfilling aspirations and consequent frustrations of this middle class, writes marvelously on this theme.

Lata, is the central character in the fictional system. She is first seen at the wedding of her sister Savita to Pran Kapoor. Lata is a student of English Literature at the University of Brahmpur, an invented city on the Ganges in the invented state of Purva Pradesh. She has a quick mind and is quite well read, though somewhat immature about life and relationships. Lata questions the idea of an arranged marriage like that of her sister where the couple knows nothing at all about each other. Her attitude is typical of the young Indian population after the separation of India from the British.

Lata is the ideal young woman, beautiful, educated and above all sensible. Her choice of a husband is guided largely by good sense and practical wisdom. She may be said to represent all that is held in high esteem by Seth, for it is through Lata that he projects the theme of sensibility in love, as it is only sound judgement that can take her to her cherished goal in a society and milieu that is undergoing tremendous change. Lata represents the purest form of human love which is one of Seth's major concerns.

Lata's mother had commenced the odyssey of finding a suitable *khatri* match for her daughter by invoking the topic at Savita's wedding and writing to all her relatives across newly independent India. But fate had a few roadblocks in Mrs Mehra's plan. With her 'modern' and 'forward' friend Malati Trivedi, Lata stumbles across one of the suitors Kabir in a bookshop. Kabir Durrani, a strikingly handsome, curly haired, cricket-freak eager to join the Diplomatic Services is a student at Brahmpur University. He is the son of Dr Durrani, an unorthodox Mathematics Professor at the University.

Lata's marriage creates two main problems which are essentially Indian; one is the looks of the girl and as already indicated the status of the family, which presupposes economic and social situation. Lata is deficient in both the aspects. As regards the looks of the girl, it is very much evidenced in the words of Lata to Malati, her friend, "I am not all that fair either, and will therefore find it impossible to find a suitable husband."(124)

It is a ridiculous paradox that while considering a marriage alliance, Indians have forever been besotted with the complexion of a girl more than the appearance. It is even funny for most of the would-be husbands and in-laws demand fair rather a milky white complexion in a hot country like India. Apart from hypocrisy, it reveals the boorishness of the patriarchal society that in spite of economic and social advancement.

It is likely to breed insecurity and subordination of women in the society governed by man's whims and fancies.

Lata, though an individual, is mainly the type of the intelligent woman living in the post-independence India. The very fact that Lata's story is placed in the wide canvass of the socio-political history of the fifties suggests her status as primarily a social being. She is almost always defined in relation to other people, like her mother or friends.

Even her personal attitudes have a strong cultural echo. They are not mere personal idiosyncrasies but authentic social attitudes.

Viewed thus, her marriage does not dwindle into an anti-romantic marriage of convenience but rather it becomes the fully responsible gesture of a socially aware individual. Thus Lata's character is a two dimensional one like many others in the novel. Lata is a victim of hypocritical Indian Society which, on one hand eulogizes the women to the pedestal of the revered selfless woman and on the other hand opposes and humiliates.

All these facts of life make Mrs.Rupa Mehra desperate and restless. To find a suitable boy, she comes to Mr.Sahagal, her sister's husband. There Lata gets a shock of her life when he tries to sexually assault her. Sexual molestation has been a phenomenon in our society since a long time.

Even today also, when women are emancipated, the existence of sexual molestation is a fact. Seth's Lata is a heroine of India in 1950s, when women had no choice but to tolerate the facts of their life. The women rightly or wrongly are leading their lives, believing in a great moral order. Seth suggests it, as a possible succour to such women as it helps them in drawing a great strength and spiritual sustenance.

It is evinced with Mrs.Rupa Mehra's acts as she feels 'He', i.e., her late husband, is still there like the unseen God, protecting her and giving solace in the anxious moments.

Mrs. Mahesh Kapoor is an extremely pious lady, and remains at peace, silently bearing the brunt of the family members' misdeeds and performing her puja and tending her garden. These kind of women, despite their helplessness in reconciling the demand of self and society do their duties and emerge victorious.

The lives of these women remain enmeshed in the domestic space of the family houses and they lack identity. It is a feminist view now-a-days. But Seth has presented an authentic picture of India in 1950s when traditional women could not transgress the feminine bounds in those days.

Marriage quest begins in the life of Lata through Kabir Durrani. Lata is enchanted by Kabir's boyish charm whereas Kabir is captivated by the depth of Lata's eyes. Though a non-Khatri Hindu, Lata falls in love with him, thinking him to be a suitable husband but Kabir's insistence on marrying her after two years clinches the issue "Two years, I think. First I have to finish my degree, after that I'm going to apply to get into Cambridge or may be take the exam "(186).

When Kabir insists Lata to wait for two years until he gets a job, Lata replies, "I'll be married off in two years, you're not a girl. You don't understand, my mother might not even let me come back to Brahampur." (125). This shows the girl's priority is for love than job. Lata's reply was instantaneous because she knows quite well that her mother never accepts Kabir who is neither of their caste nor is he employed. Moreover, Seth himself does not to approve of Kabir as a suitable boy for Lata as he is not decisive.

Kabir's rejection of Lata brings out another extremely important dimension concerning Indian society of 1950s. Kabir is a Muslim. A Hindu-Muslim marriage is impossibility. The novel abounds with examples of self-destructive passion, as in the case of Rasheed or Maan. It is tempting to conclude that Lata lacks the heroic spirit to plunge into life and love and passion for Kabir is all that; it is likely that she has discovered a Hindu identity for herself, which while allowing for intimate friendships between Hindus and Muslims, stops short of marriage.

Much to the chagrin of Mrs. Mehra starts a stubborn affair between the two literature geeks. Cupid-cum Vikram Seth strikes Lata so mercilessly that she is swooped into a mental vertigo of love and passion. All limitations are transcended when she unflinchingly pleads Kabir to elope with her as this match would never be approved by her mellow mother.

Kabir, being the reasonable one of the two refuses, which is taken by Lata as a sign of Kabir's convenient amity. But it has to be noted that despite Kabir's refusal, he adores Lata zealously and asks her to wait for him till he joins the Indian Foreign Services. To add to Lata's wretchedness, Mrs Mehra discovers her daughter with 'that Muslim boy', and Lata is straight away transported to Arun's swanky pad in Sunny Park, Calcutta.

Seth is greatly critical of such intolerance and ironically brings out the hypocrisy and sycophancy of a few selfish and power hungry people. And this relationship is more than probable that Seth had to forbid this union of Kabir and Lata, so as to emphasize his vision of communal harmony expressed in the novel through the relationship of Maan and Firoz or that of Mahesh Kapoor and the Nawab Sahib of Baitar.

They were all good friends, then problems separate them, but even when they finally come together and become friends again, "no one knew what to talk about."(132). Viewed like that, it will be insane for Lata to marry Kabir. Anyway it will be safer not to stress her Hindu identity too much, but accept the structural reason that it emphasizes the recurring idea of the book that Hindu-Muslim harmony, though highly desirable is still a practical impossibility.

The secularism of India has been regarded a matter of great pride as one tends to show great tolerance towards all religions. And yet, the reality is that this secular framework of India becomes a vulnerable target of the scathing attacks of a few fanatics who place their religion over and above, even nationality. So Lata's rejection of Kabir is to be seen as artistic need necessary for maintaining the coherence of the novel.

When man loses something his search for a better alternative begins. Amit Chatterjee, a second suitor is to enter Lata's life, though not in the strict sense of the term. He is a gifted, intelligent, witty, but eccentric and materialistically spoilt poet from Calcutta. Amit is Meenakshi's elder brother and hence enters Lata's life more as a relative and a friend rather than as a suitor. To the broken hearted Lata, who is in terrible need of a diversion, Amit's intelligence, wit and concern all combine to bring out a cheerful and carefree Lata to the fore.

Gradually Amit gets attracted by Lata's charm, innocence and simplicity. Seth has made Amit's wooing of Lata at par with Kabir's wooing, though not as passionate, as Amit is very far from being a passionate person.

It is interesting to note that Amit's wooing comes in the form of a poem, the tone of which is controlled and careful, the over tune touched with logic, and the title smacks of irony being directly borrowed from Swift–a composition that has a delightful play between passion on the one hand and witty scepticism on the other, a reminder of the metaphysical particularly Marvel

> As you have asked for black and white, May I send
> these lines to you in the tacit hope you might take my type at least
> as true. Let this distance disappear and our hearts approach from far
> till we come to be as near as acrostically we are. (1288)

Advances made by Amit Chatterjee towards Lata is abruptly stopped mid-way by her mother who instantly dislikes the Chatterjees. She says:" I have no intention of accepting things as they come, said Mrs. Rupa Mehra, the unsavory vision of sacrificing yet another of her children on the altar of the Chatterjees making her flush with indignation."(482) then, she shows her dislikes for Amit: "She looked at Amit, and thought: Poet, Wastrel! He has never earned an honest rupee in his life. I will not have all my grandchildren speaking Bengali."(486). Parents always search for a prospective groom who must be wealthy to keep their family rich and happy.

In the case of Kabir and Amit, it is Lata who has found out suitable boys for herself but Kabir does not sense the difficulty of Lata born and brought up in a conservative family, presided over by Mrs. Mehra and Amit is good for nothing, in the eyes of Mrs. Mehra for he is a poet and poets are dreamers. Lata does not like Amit and she rejects him on the ground that he is too much like for them to have a smooth domestic life, and also more important is, responsibilities have no real value for him in the long run. He can always be a good friend but never a good husband.

Haresh enters Lata's life as the third suitor. Haresh enters Lata's life as the suitable boy selected after a good deal of research work by Mrs. Rupa Mehra. But he is ironically portrayed by Seth as somebody who is socially awkward and unlettered in the sophisticated life. Nevertheless, he is acceptable to Lata because he is sincere, hard working, honest, brave, out-spoken, broad-minded, and democratic and, a staunch supporter of the family tradition.

Lata is in love with Haresh. His unaffected ways and sincere concern for everybody unconsciously endears him towards Lata, and to Lata this kind of steady affection looks are far more enduring than the desperate emotions she feels for Kabir. She chooses the flickering but steady light of the star over the blinding but temporary brilliance of the lighting.

Though Haresh is no handsome, mysterious stranger who sweeps Lata off her feet, yet there is sense of adventure and mystery in losing herself in the world, a world populated by people who are as unreal to her as Haresh is a reality. And the challenge of facing a totally different mode of life, with a man she likes and trusts a man "as solid as a pair of Goodyear welted shoes" (1292) is an attraction by itself.

Mrs. Mehra liked Haresh, her first impression of him was that he was shorter than she had expected. The next when he opened his mouth to speak was that he had been chewing paan. In fact paan did not go at all well with her idea of a husband. Later on she frankly said to Haresh : " Haresh, I think we should meet and talk a little more before I make up my mind finally. It's the most important decision of my life. I need to be completely sure." (1146)

Finally when Lata accepts Haresh without consulting her mother. She seems to have made a choice of her own. But Haresh was, from the very beginning, her mother's choice; further, no sooner was Lata's decision made public than the mother lost no time in accepting him. After Lata's wedding she tells Varun that he too "will marry a girl I choose" (1343), implying that Lata has done so. Thus the match was as much the mother's choice as it was the daughter's.

Similarly, the title, A Suitable Boy, may be taken to suggest that Haresh is only one of the suitable boys, that Kabir and Amit are perhaps equally suitable. The uncertainty regarding the rightness of her choice implies that it will be as much difficult for the reader to arrive at the right answer, as it will be for Lata to choose 'the' suitable boy. Just as Lata chooses 'a' suitable boy, the reader may choose 'a' suitable reading, 'the' suitable reading being non-existent or virtually impossible.

In deciding to marry Haresh, Lata has rejected Amit and Kabir. Amit is warm and friendly, and Lata likes and respects him. But she cannot even contemplate a marriage with him, because "we are too alike", she tells Malati (1296). She can reject his proposal without losing his friendship. But he is also Arun's brother-in-law; to marry him is to be near her brother Arun whom she cannot tolerate: "To live five minutes away from him would be the ultimate lunacy" (1297)

Arun, with his British accent and his prestigious position with Bentsen & Pryce, is a vain and empty man, an anglicized Indian basking in the reflected glory of a setting empire-the typical brown sahib under the colonial hangover. In rejecting Amit who writes only in English, she is also rejecting, though indirectly, the colonial subservience to the departed yet lingering conqueror.

Her decision to accept Haresh with his habit of paan and his unenglish English is finalized soon after receiving a letter from Arun advising her to the contrary.

Thus her rejection of Amit and acceptance of Haresh, both being a rejection of Arun and the superficial values he embodies, proves at least to a certain extent, her sense of national identity, her pride in being an Indian, and her refusal to hang on to the colonial values. Thus it becomes clear that her 'personal' motives become significant mainly in the social context.

Her attitude to Kabir is more complex. Even after promising to marry Haresh, she thinks of Kabir longingly; she cannot be sure that she is doing the right thing in rejecting Kabir. "Even now I almost feel it's he who's left me and I can't bear it" (1332). Apart from her attachment to her family and her unwillingness to hurt her mother, she cannot comprehend the violent nature of his passion and jealousy. The book abounds with examples of self-destructive passion, as in the case of Rasheed or Maan.

Here, mention may be made of Sudhir Kakar a psychoanalyst. He says of the social organization of an Indian family system as: "The mother functions as the external ego of the child for a much longer period than is customary in the West and many of the ego functions concerned with reality are later transferred from mother to the family and other social institutions.

Caste and clan are more than brotherhoods; they define the individual completely. The individual is never of his own; he is always fundamentally a member of his group within a complex apparatus of rules, rituals or taboos. Every detail of behaviour is regulated. relationships are codified."(131)

This clearly explains Mrs.Rupa Mehra becoming extremely over bearing to the extent of almost losing her sanity. She has to be continuously vigilant as far as Lata's actions and wishes are concerned. The Indian mother is invariably very protective, rather over-protective. Even though Lata accepts Haresh, she has inner attraction towards Kabir.

For the sake of the family and society, Lata discards her love. Generally, Indian woman are brought up in such protective and comfortable atmosphere that it requires immense courage and strength of mind to break away from that family bond. First, they give a preference to their family member's sentiments than their feelings and emotions. Here Lata's love quest towards Kabir ends up.

According to R.K.Gupta, the character of Lata is a failure because, "Lata's final choice of Haresh is disconcertingly anti-climatic. We never learn what makes her choose Haresh rather than Amit or Kabir."(137). After Lata's wedding, her mother tells Varun that he too "will marry a girl I choose" (138) implying that Lata has done so. Thus the match was as much the mother's choice as it was the daughter's.

'Love at first sight' has not only been rejected but also the consequences of such love have been revealed in the novel. Arun Mehra had married the vivacious Meenakshi because he was attracted by her physical beauty and later Meenakshi's coquetry with Billy Irani reveals the superficiality of a love marriage based on passion alone.

Maan and Saeeda Bai carry forward their illicit relationship but meet its tragic end. Lata on the other hand, charms Amit and Haresh due to her simplicity and intelligence. Haresh's instant opinion about Lata is: "This girl is intelligent without arrogance and attractive without vanity."(139)

In Indian communities there is a strong bonding among its members. No family is alone. The marriages, the child birth, the festivals or the mourning on death are heralded by meetings of different families and friends. These occasions are moments of oneness and this oneness unites families and communities and strengthens the foundation of love, chastity, caring, sharing and bonding. These are moral values which bring people closer and form the basis of Indian society and Indianess.

The novel is the best example of continuation of the tradition of arranged marriage as true to the times of 1950s. In India, marriage is a well established institution which presupposes certain customs and rites, various values, issues and obstacles.

Marriage in India does not merely mean the meeting of two individuals, but it signifies mixing and mingling of two families and involves respecting and understanding the customs and tradition as well as the members of each other's families.

When Lata conveys her reasons for opting for a more mature relationship with Haresh, over the possibilities of a more youthful passionate love with Kabir. Her friend Malati is horrified and cannot believe her choice. Lata finally decides to marry Haresh Khanna for pragmatic reasons. Both Amit and Kabir are impractical lovers for her and she rejects their outer life and in favour of the inner life of personal relations, actualities of material life represented by Haresh.

To help her in making up her mind, Haresh gives his paan chewing habit. He proudly asserts: "I am a practical man, and I am proud of it."(1290). She accepts him as her equal in status and superiority of intellect and wiser judgements.

She explains to Malati why she has rejected her other two suitors; "Haresh's feet touch the ground, and he has dust and sweat and a shadow. The other two are a bit too God-like and ethereal to be any good for me"(1299).

She is impressed by Haresh as being "generous, robust, optimistic, impatient, and responsible" and willing to "Mahraise" himself for her sake. (1290)

As she puts it, " Haresh is practical , he's forceful , he isn't cynical, he gets things done and he helps people without making a fuss about it"(1297). While Lata agrees that her feelings for Haresh do not have the same intensity as those for Kabir, she justifies her rejection of Kabir by quoting Clough's lines on two different kinds of human attraction. "One that merely excites, unsettles, and makes you uneasy." And the other which is "a calmer, less frantic love, which helps you to grow where you were already growing" (1299).

Lata reflects on how she has changed in the course of the year. She has also developed a different view of the realities of marriage. "Lata had begun to look at marriage with more than a disinterested eye" (877). Mr. Sahgal is abusing his daughter. The Chatteriji have a companionable marriage which is based around concern for their children.

Arun claims his marriage is based on trust but he is being deceived. The spoilt super sophisticated and glamour Meenakshi has extra martial affair and becomes pregnant. She induces a miscarriage and then continues seeing Arun's friend, Billy Irani.

While Mrs. Mahesh Kapoor is an ideal Hindu wife, or too long suffering woman, depending on our view of her, Pran and Savita make a very touching couple, they "loved each other or rather had come to do so. They both assumed, without ever needing to state it or perhaps without even thinking explicitly about it-that marriage and children were great good" (876). Lata has recognized at an earlier point that love does not necessarily rest on the choice of an individual for another individual. She realizes that Savita, who loves Pran would probably have fallen in love with any good man.

But whether it was owing to the hectoring of the mother or her overly copious love or the vision of these different families on Pran's illness or the birth of Savita's baby or all of them combined. Lata felt she had changed. The sleeping Savita was perhaps a more powerful advisor that the voluble Malati. (877). As Lata's sister has changed in status and become a mother, so Lata's view of herself has altered.

Lata looked back on her wish to elope with Kabir with a kind of amazement, even as she could not shake off her feelings for him. But where would these feelings lead? A gradual, stable attraction such as Savita's for

Pran was this not the best things for her, and for the family, and for any children that she might have? (877)

Lata has begun to think of herself not only as a student of English literature, friend of Malati, and youngest of four children, but as a possible wife and future mother. This changes her view of the sort of man she wants to marry. Malati finds Kabir's letter to teenage Lata and though Lata points out that volunteering to help after the Pul Mela disaster was not the action of a teenager, she too is unsatisfied with his letter.

The character of Kabir, in comparison to Haresh, remains sketchy: he studies, plays cricket, and acts well. He also goes to see his mentally ill mother and this, as well as the help he gives at the Pul Mela, speaks of an admirable sense of duty. However, he still seems very young, the ambitions he speaks to Lata are those of a single man, and not one ready to settle down and have family. In comparison, Haresh has many more connections with the rest of the society with Kedarnath and Bhaskar, the Jatav community, Kalpana Gaur, and his own large family in Delhi.

Arun's letter, in which he tries to persuade Lata not to marry Haresh, has the predictable effect of making Lata and the reader like Haresh more. Most of Arun's reasons are based on social snobbery. When Arun talks about his own marriage as "a happy one based on mutual affection and trust"(1292). Haresh both by his erstwhile constancy to the unobtainable Simran, and his openness to Lata and her mother about his previous love, has shown himself to be trustworthy. The steadiness of his affection for Lata and his positive outlook also recommend him as the right choice for Lata.

Lata recognizes the effectiveness of such relationships. She slowly develops the ponderings on Indian values and familial responsibility. Despite all her annoyance and disobedient approach towards her mother, she understands the cause behind her mother's stable anxiety that made her rather over-caring and over-protective. Lata comprehends that as a true Indian parent, her mother could not overlook her familial responsibility.

Lata's mother was concerned about Pran's physical condition because of his asthmatic attacks. She was again anxious about Savita who was about to deliver the baby and she was continually worried about Lata's marriage and Varun's job. She is very much at the rudder of dealings and remainds tireless in all circumstances. So she deserves all the admiration and esteem.

Seth definitely appears as a thinker while integrating such serious but essential component of Indian social life.

The characterization shows Seth's deep insight, honesty and truthfulness in portraying an ordinary Indian woman's gradual development towards maturity. At the beginning of the novel, Lata is nineteen year old and at the end, she is twenty. But the difference between the nineteen year old Lata and the twenty year old Lata is not just simply one year.

Within this one year Lata grows from a moody and willful girl to a woman who realizes and understands responsibilities and thereby acts accordingly. Lata's characterization also reveals to us a great deal of Vikram Seth's novel ideologies. In her search for a groom, Lata chooses Haresh not because of her mother's compulsions, but because of the simple reason that she wants to marry somebody like Haresh.

At the time Lata accepts Haresh's proposal, her mother is having second thoughts about him because of some derogatory remarks made by her friends and relatives, concerning his involvement in the shoe business. Arun has also arrogantly rejected Haresh, on the plea that he is socially inferior to them, and therefore will be more of an embarrassment to their family.

Another central character in this novel is Maan Kapoor whose marital chase for Saeeda Bai. Maan is the son of a powerful Hindu member of the senate. Firoz Kahn, the best friend of Maan. He is the son of a powerful and wealthy land owner. From Childhood, they have been friends and it is clearly hinted at in several places in the book that they have been lovers.

For Maan it appears that their sexual encounters are for the most part innocent boyhood dalliances along the lines of boarding school shenanigans. But for Firoz, it is clear from the first scene that they share that his feelings for Maan go much deeper. Although Maan is also very affectionate to Firoz and seems to allow Firoz to initiate tender sexual encounters between them rather happily.

Even if Maan is in love with Firoz, he longs for Saeeda Bai. Maan's love quest is towards Saeeda Bai. He has a sexual obsessive affair with an older female courtesan, Saeeda Bai. He cannot get her out of his head; he messes up his business and his relationship with his family because of his sexual obsession for her.

Maan also essentially tortures Firoz with his endless talk of Saeeda Bai, all of her charm, his longing for her and his love for her. Firoz's unhappiness seems to be a combination of jealously and outright concern for how Maan is messing up his life with the affair. At the same time, Firoz finds himself attracted to Saeeda Bai's young sister, Tasneem. He craves for Tasneem. When Saeeda Bai discovers Firoz's passion towards Tasneem, she admits her past to Firoz that Tasneem is his half sister in the way of Firoz's father Nawab raped Saeeda Bai at the age of fifteen in a drunken moment.

Tasneem thereby is not Saeeda's sister but "The child she had conceived in terror had carried in shame and had borne in pain "(1212). Firoz's attraction towards Tasneem comes to end on hearing the past.

When Maan sees Firoz with Saeeda Bai, he assumes Firoz and Saeeda Bai are lovers. In the angry mood, he stabs Firoz in the stomach and he nearly dies. Maan is put into prison in the cause of love. Saeeda Bai realizes that she truly and deeply loves Maan. Maan finally gets to see Firoz, and there is a touching reconciliation scene where Maan presses his forehead to Firoz's and cries.

In the mean time, Firoz knows that Maan did not intend to kill him, but was insane with jealousy, and Firoz has always accepted that Maan loses control of himself and his emotions too easily. The intensely jealous Maan suspecting his friend's involvement with Saeeda, stabs Firoz and then stumbles into the dark of the night, covered with blood.

Maan is arrested and charged with dangerous assault. The shock of his arrest causes his mother to die from a stroke. Then comes the dramatic courtroom scene in which Firoz pleads a memory lapse and does not offer evidence against Maan. Finally Maan is compelled to leave Brahmpur in such unhappy spirits.

There are a section of people in the society who long for identity, their search for recognition and honour is pathetic one such character is Saeeda Bai. Her quest for identity evokes sympathy. Saeeda Bai is a woman of lower level, one without social dignity, without resources; she has therefore to resort to the temporary pleasures of drink and sex.

Seth brings in the contrast of the sacred versus disrespectful love anti-thesis. Saeedi Bai plays a rotten game while Lata goes in search of meaning of true, noble love. There is a void in Saeeda Bai's life so she is in quest of meaning and hence symbolic of man's existential loneliness in the Universe.

Saeeda Bai's inner solitude, the meaninglessness of her glittering but caged life, the lack of emotional stability and her passing for a happy woman is another aspect of social life that forms the novel's pattern of contrast. Saeeda Bai says of the bareness of her life:

> Now look at me ... I still feel young... I am waiting
>
> to spend the evening with this disgustingly ugly man
>
> who is fifty five years old who picks his nose and belches
>
> and who is going to be drunk even before he gets here.....
>
> what about my feelings? (119)

Maan's illicit relationship with Saeeda Bai ultimately spells his ruin and while he stakes his reputation and future for Saeeda Bai. She never marries him. A courtesan can never be accepted as a respectable daughter-in-law in modern Indian society. Seth does not restore what cannot be socially accepted in a convention-bound society and hence he may be said to take a very practical and realistic view of sex and marriage.

But Saeeda Bai cannot ever hope to regain her lost position. Her life is barren. She is determined to protect Tasneem from the outside world. But Tasneem is well aware that she will ultimately "change these four walls for a different four" (114). Music learned by Saeeda Bai has been directed towards making her a more desirable object for male consumption.

Saeeda Bai receives a regular monthly stipend from the Nawab of Baitar as a compensation for her.

In spite of her relations with Maan, she is essentially a lonely woman who finds escape from boredom in liquor and sex. It is only with Maan that life comes to have some meaning for her but even so she is far from satisfied.

Her building up of a paradise with Maan shows that she has found an ideal companion in him. But their separation again leaves her as lonely as she ever was.

For all the importance which the sexual passions have in motivating human behavior in *A Suitable Boy,* it is extraordinary what anachronistic Victorian delicacy Vikram Seth displays on the subject. None of the erotic encounters between Maan Kapoor and the courtesan musician Saeeda Bai are evoked neither is the homoerotic scene between Maan Kapoor and Firoz Nawab in the hills fortress of his father.

The drunken rape of Saeeda Bai when she was only fifteen by the Nawab Sahib is only revealed after the tragic climax and is then also referred to very indirectly. There are almost no physical descriptions of bodies as the cause of sexual allure, not even with the adulterous vamp Meenakshi. If anything, the adulterous meetings between Meenakshi and poor, frightened Billy are done as a force on the domineering female vamp.

Vikram Seth seems interested in the social aspects of sexual relations, not their physical intimacy. His tasteful restraint contrasts with the heavy-breathing explicitness of much contemporary Western fiction.

Indeed the magical masseur says it is all on Seth's behalf when he states: "family life with children is a comedy, today, yesterday and tomorrow" (798).

It is not that Seth's characters do not experience sexual passion; it is that, passion is deliberately marginalized by the narrator as part of the moral contrivance of the novel. The readers hear only of the confusion, the anguish and ultimately the misery of those characters who have not managed to control their passion.

The Nawab Sahib feels lifelong shame and makes lifelong payments to his natural daughter whom he has never seen or acknowledged. Saeeda Bai is left in utter misery and solitude at the end after Maan Kapoor has finally renounced his obsessive and criminal passion for her.

Ustad Khan and Firoz khan both suffer through their yearning for Saeeda Bai's beautiful daughter Tasneem. The most unsuitable boy, Kabir's appearances are limited, after his blissful but chaste break of dawn boat ride with Lata, to scenes of anguish and confusion, until his final appearance as a despairing rejected lover by the side of the river at the end of the novel.

Finally, Rasheed, the sternly righteous, self-sacrificing Rasheed, who out of duty marries his elder brother's widow, is driven by subconscious guilty passion for his student Tasneem into paranoid schizophrenia and eventually to destitution and suicide on the bank of the same river at Brahmpur.

It is these scenes of despair to which Vikram Seth devoted his evocative skills and they are all reinforcements for his moral contrivance in the novel to persuade readers of the sinister evil of sexual passion which these characters seek. The gentle and constant marital affection of Savita for Pran or Mrs.Kapoor for Mahesh Kapoor are held up by contrast as a persuasive counterpoint.

The Kapoor clan is headed by Mr.Mahesh Kapoor, Revenue Minister in the S.S. Sharma ministry of Purva Pradesh, a Nehruite. His wife is deeply religious, superstitious and conservative. His daughter Veena is married into the Tandon family with Kedarnath Tandon. His elder son Pran Kapoor, an asthmatic lecturer in English at Brahmpur University, is married into the Mehra family, with Savita Kapoor. Except Mahesh Kapoor and Maan Kapoor, the whole family is traditionalist.

Mahesh Kapoor is also a politician, the Minister of Revenue of the state of Purva Pradesh who craves for power. After spending some time in British Jails during the struggle for independence, Mahesh Kapoor has bent into someone who likes power. That is why he enjoys being a Minister. It gives him the chance to imitate what he had been showing to another beneath him. It is a kind of revenge: Pran had never been able to realize why people loved power, but he received it as a fact of life.

Mahesh Kapoor is the chief of the family. He controls the whole thing and each one as the master of the house. Most perhaps his commanding approach is a mirror image of the political on the personal. He comes across tough power relations first under the British rule. Then he begins to apply it to his independent government and as a result its effects are felt back at home.

His relationship with his wife is exactly power relations in which the male is dominant and the female obedient. That is why Lata thinks that the name of their house, 'Prem Nivas', is ironic. Because it means "the abode of love" (16) but the people in the house do not have a love relationship at all.

Mahesh Kapoor sees his wife as a useless creature. He treats his wife as the British treated Indians. But she gives respect to her husband. "When referring to her husband, often called him 'Minister Sahib'.Sometimes, in Hindu, she even called him 'Pran's father'. To refer to him by name would have been unthinkable. Even 'my husband' was unacceptable to her (191). Mahesh Kapoor always addresses his wife in demeaning and insulting way such as "that weak-willed woman" (7).

A man like Mahesh Kapoor, who abuses his wife, is usually passive and dependent individual. He finds it difficult to express the emotions and to deal with the anger in nonviolent ways. Often he did not have a close bond with his mother. He has no close, warm, intimate relationship with a woman at all. A man who abuses his wife often has a low self esteem and the wife does as well. Power and control are also essential features in the dynamics of spouse abuse.

In *A Suitable Boy* the main plot line is like that of *The Golden Gate*. It is centered on the question of finding a suitable partner. The conflict between individual desires and conditions imposed by the larger community is seen in Lata's conflict over the choice of husband and her final decision; Lata's choice is a boy most suited to her own culture and her place in society. The novel reveals whether the heroine Lata will submit to her mother Rupa Mehra's arrangement, or she will follow her own heart, even if that means defying not only her mother, but also all barriers of caste and religion.

Seth proved himself a prose novelist of great strength and vision, a novelist of quality and commitment endowed with a capacity to sweep the great tradition of the novel in English into his broad perspective. Every work of literature creates its own world. Like Henry Fielding, who stressed the idea of the novel as a comic epic in prose and sought to encompass the whole of the eighteenth century social life in his works.

In a volume exceeding thirteen hundred pages, Seth sets out to bring the entire post-independence India into his fictional vision. As a writer, Seth is conversant with life on various social levels. Well acquainted with both the high and the inferior sector of mankind, he portrays the mid-twentieth century society in all its diversity which provided him with a fictional technique of contrasting characters and their life styles with remarkable aesthetic effect.

It is the early winter of 1950 and India has been independent from British colonial rule for three years. The narrative is largely set in the fictitious city of Brahmpur. Seth has acknowledged Brahmpur as a combination of different geographic locations known to him Patna. Brahmpur lies on the banks of the river Ganges. However the meandering Ganges does not really symbolize the unity of the Indian nation state as some critics have suggested. Since Seth's focus is restricted to an Indian north of the Vindhya. The narrative shifts scenes to Patna, Calcutta, Banaras and Allahabad also.

In Indian society girl children could not aspire more, however good looking and educated they are the anxiety of parents in getting them married to a suitable groom is always there. Even before the girl blooms into womanhood, the search for a prospective husband begins. This aspect is invariably present across the length and breadth of India.

Marriage is an important social institution in Indian society and searching for a bride and groom is considered as important and serious factor in one's life and responsibility of parents.

After Savita is married, Mrs.Rupa Mehra turns towards finding a bridegroom for her younger daughter Lata. Seth's thematic fixation is multifold. But Mrs.Mehra's quest for 'a suitable boy' remains a connecting strand from the beginning to the end of the novel. For the widowed Mrs. Mehra, the task of arranging Lata's marriage is a commitment ordained by social norms. Mrs. Mehra must take into serious consideration issues of religion, caste and social standing.

Traditionally, marriages are, as the fictional Mrs. Mehra in *A Suitable Boy* rightly states, arranged by the parents of a boy or girl, and in respectable middle class families, where the average age of marriage lies now in the mid-twenties, arranged marriages are seen as the norm. The search for a suitable match is considered a parental obligation, although it can also become a burden, but in times when many children seek out their own partner, it is increasingly constructed as a crucial parental privilege.

In private discussions young people in particular would speak very emotionally about their expectations regarding love and marriage and would often use a lot of vocabulary that is associated with companionate marriage, for instance the English word 'soul mate' representing an ideal partner. The themes of conjugality, love and changes in expectations towards marriage form part of the fabric of family life in Calcutta middle class families, just as they dominate the narrative of Vikram Seth's monumental novel.

Seth confesses that he had initially intended to write a short book of about two hundred and fifty pages concentrating mainly on Lata's or her mother's search for a suitable match for her. But he adds her "having begun it with a wedding and having lots of characters take part in that wedding. I realized that I was quite interested in the individual lives of these people and have they come together again. So having opened the gate a bit wider I realized I was writing a different kind of a book". (12)

Seth employs a quasi-historical structure and focuses on the first few years after Indian independence leading up to the first general elections of 1952. The multilinker-narrative follows chronological time. This was a period of tumulus economic, political and communal upheavals. When Justice Chatterji compares the list of names of Judges on the first page of the All India Reports of 1948 with that of the previous year of 1947, he notices the absence of the names of a large number of British and Muslim colleagues.

The judge sadly reflects that " ... in macrocosm these two pages reflect the passage of an empire and the birth of two countries from the idea tragic and ignorant that people of different religions cannot live together in one"....

"Who'd have thought", he asks himself. "... that things would have changed as much and swiftly as they had?"(468-69). The seemingly uneventful narrative of social manners and lifestyles of the Indian middle class is offset with detailed accounts of social and political crises. "The nuts and bolts of political demographics" as Field puts it: "run through the novel set against the background of the partition". (46)

A Suitable Boy takes us into the richly imagined world of four large extended families and spins a compulsively readable tale of their lives and loves. This sprawling novel tells the stories of four Indian families, the Mehra, the Khans, the Kapoors and the Chatterjee. The interwoven stories of four families linked by marriage form the background for this marital quest.

Vikram Seth uses this search to explore the conflict between the older generation, for whom marriage should be arranged to the best advantage of the family, and the younger generation who feel that love is search for that suitable boy. He shows the life of ordinary people who caught up in a web of love and ambition, humour and sadness, prejudice and reconciliation.

The family drama of the matrimonial quest is interwoven with the politics of the post-independent India. The main interest is divided between four families and only two Lata and Maan approach the conventional heroic type. The main part of the story is the search for a suitable boy. The sub part of the story is the academic skullduggery, the political parallelism between Nehru and Tandon, on the one hand, and the political rift between L.N. Agarwal and Mahesh Kapoor, on the other, Saeeda Bai and Maan all help the main story to stand on surer and firmer footing.

Mehras are led by Mrs.Rupa Mehra and Late Rahubir Mehra , Lata, Savita and Pran(son of Mahesh Kapoor and son-in-law of Mrs. Mehra) , Varun are on the side of Mrs.Mehra. They are traditionalists. Arun Mehra and his wife,

Meenakshi Mehra (daughter of Justice Chatterjee) represent modernity. From the beginning, Mrs.Rupa Mehra informing Lata, that like her elder sister Savita, she too will marry a boy of her choice.

Lata's reaction to this maternal is a typical example of any other young Indian girl's reaction. In the sense typically there is no reaction, only indifference. Lata has no attraction towards arranged marriages, but she knows that she has to have one because she can never hurt the emotions of her family members by going against their decisions, mainly her mother. "Because of my family," said Lata, "however much they irritate me and constrain me I cannot give them up. I know that now so much has happened I can't give up my mother."(166)

Generally, Indian women before marriage are brought up in such a caring and calm atmosphere that it requires vast courage and power of mind to break away from that strong family bond. And there is always this risk that once you break free; it is almost next to impossible to get back into the fold. This holds true even now, even in the twenty-first century, while in the 1950s, the period when Seth's story is enacted, it was almost unthinkable.

However, an anonymous reader responding to the novel online suggests, quite rightly, that perhaps only an Indian reader would really understand Lata's ultimate decision: "Lata's final choice is one you didn't want her to choose, but would expect if you know India."Unlike Amit who can afford to remain unmarried or Kabir who plans to pursue his studies abroad, such choices are not really open to Lata.

It is in 1951, she is nineteen and she knows that in another two years she will definitely be married off. She therefore opts for what she believes is the most sensible choice in the circumstances. Haresh's calmer; less frantic love will allow her to grow at her own pace.

She is confident that Haresh will encourage her to teach if she so desires, as he hates to see other people's talents wasted. It is the ideal domesticity of Savita's home, that Lata must aspire for, and she sees Haresh as being in position to provide her with the same. (1332).

Lata is not marrying Haresh; she is marrying a symbol of what Vikram Seth would like to proclaim as, his hope for a new India–an ambitious, pragmatic, anti-snobbish, working class, self-made Indian man. This is what most women long for, their search for an ideal man. For this Lata is prepared to go without the ecstasy of passion because this means she can opt for self control and rational calm and social order through pre marital chastity and strict monogamy. She negates passion because according to Seth, it terrifyingly transforms the individual as an inevitable concomitant of suffering and confusion, and in the end wreaks destruction and despair.

All the plots are centered about a search- Mrs.Mehra's search for a suitable boy, Mr. Mahesh Kapoor's search for political and social stability and equality, the Nawab's pursuit to keep his land and Justice Chatterji's quest to get one of his sons to take care of family matters in between the entire Chatterji-family quest for the meaning of life, or finding a suitable husband, or getting everything your heart desires. .

In other words, the book centers on the concept of "pursuit".

It is however, not surprising that a novel about this particular period concentrates on the issue of a quest, since Indian in this era is trying to establish its own national identity.

10. MARITAL DISHARMONY OF MAYA IN ANITA DESAI'S CRY, THE PEACOCK

Marriage is a basic institution in every society. It is the recognized social institution, not only for establishing and maintaining the family, but also for creating and sustaining the ties of kinship. Family is the most important primary group in society. Family and marriage are considered to be the two pillars of the society.

In India, traditionally, marriage has been hallowed as sacred. Once the couple enters into the bond of marriage, the relationship is considered perpetual till the death does them apart. The current social scene of the modern Indian society shows a great change in the traditional idea of marriage. They drift apart when they are unable to sort out their problems which result in the strain and tension in their relationship.

Though the traditional conceptions regarding the status and role of husband and wife are slowly changing in contemporary Indian society, the tradition oriented conceptions still largely prevail. Today's married working women are facing a great challenge to maintain a balance between personal and professional life. The process of industrialization and urbanization has brought about socio psychological changes in the attitudes and values of the people of this country, especially among the urban population. The opening-up of endless opportunities to married women outside their homes has brought about a widespread feminine unrest.

Marital Discord is a very effective stressor that can prompt individuals to enter stages or engage in behavior that will lead them to have psychotic or organic features. It is a significant predictor of subsequent delinquency and depressive symptoms for married couples.

It is evident that marital problems are more likely to cause depression than depression is to cause marital problems.

Divorce is the final tragic denouement of family disorganization. More young people are filing for divorce, some in the first year of their marriage. Most of these divorces are mutual consent petitions. Contrary to what prevailed earlier, more women are initiating divorce proceedings. The society seems to be accepting the fact that divorcees need companionship.

Marital discord can have a negative consequence on developing children. One of the most awful things to a child is the possibility that their parents may break up. In the heat of marital discord, many people fail to distinguish the intense fear aggravated in their children. The emotional withdrawal of the couple can have either of the two effects on children: Firstly, children become fearful of parents disengagement leading to an eventual breakup of the family home. Secondly, children learn emotional disengagement as a strategy for dealing with challenging interpersonal situations.

In marriage two individuals with different backgrounds come together. Their attitudes, mindset, and thinking cannot be expected to be same. It takes some time to understand each other. Isolation, lack of communication, irritating habits, and expectations are the main reasons which lead to marital discord. The concept of marital discord dominates the contemporary literature. It is one of the fundamental themes in the works of Vikram Seth, Nayantara Sahgal , Anita Desai and others.

Among the post-independent Indo-English writers, Anita Desai holds a prominent place because of the immense popularity she commands as a novelist of human predicament of anxiety, frustration and loneliness in the insensitive and inconsiderate contemporary world. Her novels are the manifesto of female predicament.

Her preoccupation with the women's inner world, frustration and storm raging inside her mind intensify her predicament. Desai's concern with the emancipation of women is found page after page in her novels. Her central theme is the existential predicament of an individual which she projects through incompatible couple, very sensitive wife and ill-matched husband.

Anita Desai has highlighted marital discord as a serious concern in her works. In her novels, marital discord is reflective of the social parlance. Her works are directly related to social realities.

In *Cry, the Peacock,* she has portrayed the man-woman relationship and the untold sufferings of women out of the marital discord. Anita Desai symbolizes peacock to reveal and portray the anguish of Maya. Maya's position is like a trapped and caged bird.

Anita Desai's novel *Cry, the Peacock* is a family play with the theme of marital discord between Gautama and Maya. The novel is about Maya's cry for love and relationship in her loveless wedding. The Peacock's cry is an implication of Maya's distressed cry for love and life of involvement. Maya is pensive and touching, while Gautama is insensible and lucid. The growing tension between them reaches its climax when Maya kills Gautama and then commits suicide.

In *Cry, the Peacock,* Desai probes the heart of a woman who suffers from a mysterious premonition about the tragic end of her husband would die in the fourth year of their marriage. When the novel opens, Maya's marriage with Gautama is running in its fourth year and the emotional woman Maya, is just beginning to reel under the pressure of the prophecy that threatens to shatter her married life. The novelist keeps Maya's mother out of her life, since Maya has been deprived of a mother's love, this painful void in her emotional life can be one of the factor responsible for her marital discord. In

Maya's life, the only mother figure is her mother-in-law, and she too comes into her life, too late to be any help. She is sympathetic but helpless and her belated appearance shows that she is important but was not there earlier when she was most needed.

Maya's sense of insecurity is further intensified by the absence of her brother who could have been a dear childhood companion. But, from deriving a sense of security from her brother, she finds that she is living in a situation that is marked by conflict between the two people who are dearest to her father and her brother. She wants demonstrative love and does she has to loud displays of love. With her marriage not get it after marriage. Her father fixation is so great that she marries Gautama because of his friendship with her father.

After marriage she expects her husband to play as father with her. Maya does not grow up mentally which results in suffering. She has not attained emotional maturity which comes through facing facts and is content with the false nation that her husband can substitute her father and she can still behave like a child.

Gautama on the contrary, is aware of her father fixation. He tells Maya that she suffers from father fixation and until she matures rapidly, she will not be able to deal with life and will probably destroy herself in the end since passion of this sort is almost always self-consuming like any other husband Gautama expects Maya to behave like a mature person.

Maya compares Gautama to her father at every step and thus ruins her marital life completely. Perhaps, Gautama would have been better able to handle her if he had been told of her weak mental state by her father. Perhaps her father wished to keep this a secret not only from Gautama but from others as well, because such a revelation might have reduced his daughter's chances of marriage for who would willingly marry a psychic case.

Gautama fails to satisfy Maya's physical needs as well. On one occasion, in spite of her seductive postures, Gautama remains rigid and cold. On another occasion, Maya laments: "longing to be with him, be close to him...make haste in undressing....But when I went...he had closed his eyes not with mere tiredness, but in profound, invulnerable sleep, and was very far from any world of mine, however enticing"(93). Thus she remains physically dissatisfied.

When Maya's pet Toto die, Gautama does not show any regard for the sentiments and emotions. But he asks her to make tea and stop crying. Maya, who is in great shock at the death of Toto, despairs the detached attitude of Gautama. Toto was a symbol of warm, faithful and was intimately attached to her. He was a child substitute for her.

Maya feels that Gautama does not appreciate the emotional value of her desires and grief. Maya expresses her desire to go to the south to see the Kathakali dance. But Gautama looks at this curious proposal with suspicious and pushes aside her desire without caring much for the intensity of her desire.

Gautama is a faithful husband who loves and cares her in his own way yet Maya never satisfied and happy. The problem and the agony of Maya's life are accurately reflected in the significant fable of the peacock's mating ritual. The cry of peacock is the cry of the natural instinct of a woman who is unfulfilled. But such a fulfillment is denied to Maya.

She realizes that she wants Gautama's physical presence, his love and a normal life. She is capable of empathy which enables her to experience what the peacock and peahen are experiencing but this makes her feel all the more intensely that though there is an emotional arousal, there is no physical fulfillment which is the cause of her agony and also the reason for her resentment against Gautama.

Anita Desai highlights significant issues about the complexity of human relationships as a contemporary problem and human condition using various reasons leading to marital discords. In her novel, she depicts the fruitless marriage relationship which frequently leads to separation and isolation of the characters.

Most of the times, the inability of an individual to be responsive to the behavior pattern of her partner leads to tension and stress in the relationship. They struggle against strong but in vain. They become hopeless, desperate and nervous. Committing suicide, running away or living separately are the solutions visible to them. The fact that Maya turns insane and kills her husband.

Marriage is nothing but a convenience. When two souls come together through their marriage some kinds of difference is bound to be there. But the wedlock's are used to be settled blindly and without considering the attitudes, feelings and outlooks of the brides and bridegrooms, which are compelled to fail in every sphere of their conjugal lives.

Proper understanding of each other, a sense of wisdom and love for each other can make their conjugal life successful. But in India male-dominated society only women have to adjust. Adverse attitudes of the family members make the family lives, a great menace.

Anita Desai's *Cry, the Peacock* clearly exposes the psychological problems that are caused by the disintegrated marital relationship of a disharmonized woman. Marital discord is one of the important issues in our society. Anita Desai explores the grief of women living in modern society.

She presents her opinion about the human relationships and human conditions as a big contemporary problem. The key to successful marriage is true love, understanding each other, trust and adjustment.

11. MARGINALIZATION OF WOMEN IN VIKRAM SETH'S *A SUITABLE BOY*

Vikram Seth is better known as an Indian poet, novelist, travel writer, author, children's writer, biographer and also memoirist. His second novel *A Suitable Boy released* in 1993. It won Common Wealth Writers prize in 1993 and W H Smith Literary Award in 1994. It is the longest book in a single volume. The novel is divided into 19 parts with 1400 pages. Each part is described by a rhyming couplet. The story of four families over a period of 18 months as a mother searches for a suitable boy to marry her second daughter.

Women in the modern world go out to reach beyond the universe yet face many obstacles and barriers in this society i.e. due to family and religious backgrounds. Though the novel is written after independence, we still find the mentality of women the same. Vikram Seth has portrayed through his characters, women have come out in all aspects of life, and women still are not allowed to take any decision on their own. Seth has written this longest novel beautifully with many characters, especially women as he took inspiration from his own mother who became the first woman judge and later the first woman Justice of a State High Court.

The novel shows Seth's knowledge over the Indian women's way of thinking and also his mastery over literature and the physical structure of India. In *A Suitable Boy* each woman takes a different role and plays her part meaningfully and shows her ability and capability. Seth has taken a lot of effort to bring out the best qualities of women in Independent India.

We could admire the role played by a responsible widow Mrs. Rupa Mehra, the traditional souls Lata and Savita, the bold and beautiful girl

Malati, the contemporary home maker Meenakshi, The beautiful Saeeda Bai, trustworthy person Kalpana, lovable girl Veena, Submissive Mrs. Mahesh Kapoor and cute girl child Aparna.

A Suitable Boy is a landmark in Seth's career because it represents a sort of coming of age, of industrial, modern, and materialistic India. *A Suitable Boy* is set in 1950s. This story examines the interworking and travails of four families the Kapoors, the Mehras, the Chatterjis and the Khans. Two primary characters in the story are Mrs. Rupa Mehra and Lata, her marriageable but rebellious youngest daughter. Mrs. Rupa Mehra is a widow whose mission throughout the novel is to take care of family and in particular, the search for a suitable husband for Lata.

Traditionally, marriages are, as the fictional Mrs. Mehra in *A Suitable Boy* rightly states, arranged by the parents of a boy or girl, and in respectable middle class families, where the average age of marriage lies now in the mid-twenties, arranged marriages are seen as the norm. The search for a suitable match is considered a parental obligation, although it can also become a burden, but in times when many children seek out their own partner, it is increasingly constructed as a crucial parental privilege.

Across Bengali Hindu and as well as Muslim communities, biye (marriage) constitutes a life cycle ritual and is thus necessary to make a person into a full human being, a process of mental as well as physical transformation through sexual activity, reproduction and nurture.

Mrs. Rupa Mehra represents an ordinary mother's character of our society. All mothers have a wonderful dream about their daughter's marriage. They want to bring a suitable partner to their daughters with all the prosperities. The most realized and emotional character is Mrs. Rupa

Mehra who has only one mission left in life to arrange a proper marriage for her youngest daughter, Lata.

Mother and daughter are generation apart in their ideas, but not surprisingly they eventually do reach an agreement of sorts, as a result of which they find that they are closer than they had ever imagined. Mrs. Rupa Mehra is a woman who is determined to take care of her family at any cost, in fact, to take care of them even if they do not wish to be taken care of.

Mrs. Rupa Mehra is indeed a remarkable character, and not one is soon forgotten. She is vividly drawn and seems to leap off the page with energy, vitality and wit. Mrs. Rupa Mehra is the typical Indian mother, always concerned about her children and always eager to see to it that they settle well in life. And yet, behind the apparent liveliness and positive tones to the whole mother and daughter drama, there are glimpses of resentment at the limitations of an economic and social world in which women had no future but what their husbands could provide or their fathers, if they had been unlucky in the hunt.

Lata is the ideal young woman-beautiful, educated, and above all sensible. Her choice of a husband is guided largely by good sense and practical wisdom. She may be said to represent all that is held in high esteem by Seth for it is through Lata that he projects the theme of sensibility in love, as it is only sound judgment that can take her to her cherished goal in a society and milieu that is undergoing tremendous change.

Lata represents the purest form of human love which is one of Seth's major concerns. Her life of love does not exhibit strong passion or any kind of heedlessness, because Seth does not give it a heightened romantic effect to make it the central force of the story. She shows no reckless passion for her two boyfriends–Kabir Durrani and Haresh Khanna.

Seth seems to believe in Lata's surer guidance of the head and intuitive flashes of the mind, and avoids presenting a situation in which strong impulses threaten to sweep away rational faculties. Like Jane Austen's heroine Emma, Lata can just as well say "I am quite enough in love. I should be sorry to be more"(232). It is not enough to say that Lata is incapable of love; rather she is cool in both public and private life.

Probably no heroine in fiction thinks more of her lover's intelligence than of his good looks as does Seth's Lata. She adopts a rational perspective of the young man's virtues and weaknesses. In a letter to Kabir, her poet friend, she writes in a controlled rational tone:

> I have your note.....I got your letter too when I was in Calcutta. It made me think over and remember everything. I am not annoyed with you in any way; please do not think so. But I feel that there is no purpose at all in our writing or meeting. There would be a lot of pain and very little point. (ASB776)

She finally marries Haresh who is best suited to her and is approved of by her mother. She accepts him as her equal in status and superiority of intellect and wiser judgments. On the eve of her marriage, she does not indulge in idle romance but reflects on their life together.

The characterization shows Seth's deep insight, honesty and truthfulness in portraying an ordinary Indian woman's gradual development towards maturity. At the beginning of the novel, Lata is nineteen year old and at the end, she is twenty. But the difference between the nineteen year old Lata and the twenty year old Lata is not just simply one year. Within this one year Lata grows from a moody and willful girl to a woman who realizes and understands responsibilities and thereby acts accordingly.

Lata's characterization also reveals to us a great deal of Vikram Seth's novel ideologies.

In her search for a groom, Lata chooses Haresh not because of her mother's compulsions, but because of the simple reason that she wants to marry somebody like Haresh. At the time Lata accepts Haresh's proposal, her mother is having second thoughts about him because of some derogatory remarks made by her friends and relatives, concerning his involvement in the shoe business. Arun has also arrogantly rejected Haresh, on the plea that he is socially inferior to them, and therefore will be more of an embarrassment to their family.

Savita, the elder daughter of Mrs.Rupa Mehra, is very calm and adjustable type. She knows and understands her mother's pain and sufferings. She accepts her mother's decision and accepts wholeheartedly to marry Pran. She is very beautiful, obedient, and a dutiful daughter of Mrs. Rupa Mehra. Even she does not see her life partner. She sees him only during the marriage. She believes that whatever her mother does is good for her life.

Seth has written that how the women like Savita accepts the will and wish of the mother. But Lata was unable to accept this marriage and was wondering about her sister Savita and telling herself that, "Savita, it was true, would have been concerned about anyone who was suffering from anything" (14). Her husband looks very thin, black and sickly person but he is very good in nature.

Savita accepts him as her life partner and leads a very happy married life. By nature she is very accommodative and receptive. She knows her mother's burden and does not want to upset her in any way.

She has enough confidence on her mother. Seth expresses the view that beauty is not being handsome but should be handsome in their actions.

Malati is very outgoing and never loses her tongue with strangers. She is a very talkative and humorous girl. Once she passes comments on Pran a university lecturer working in the English Department who is Lata's brother-in-law "Well, he is looked rather beast-like whenever I've seen him on the university campus. Like a dark giraffe" (8) Malati is not suppressed by society like most of the other women characters in the novel. On the contrary, she can be convincing whenever she wants.

Mrs. Mahesh Kapoor is an extremely pious lady, and remains at peace, silently bearing the brunt of the family members' misdeeds and performing her puja and tending her garden. These kind of women, despite their helplessness in reconciling the demand of self and society do their duties and emerge victorious.

The lives of these women remain enmeshed in the domestic space of the family houses and they lack identity. It is a feminist view now-a-days. But Seth has presented an authentic picture of India in 1950s when traditional women could not transgress the feminine bounds in those days.

Saeeda Bai is an independent, and a very good singer. Her vocation is courtesan, it is the old custom followed throughout the world, but she loves the profession and she is satisfied with all men who come to her. She follows the tradition and the cultural rules; she is the true devotee and pious person of religion.

Though she happens to see many men in her life, she falls in love with one person Mann Kapoor and he too is infatuated by her beauty. But she refused to marry him because she is a Muslim girl and prostitute.

She advises him to marry according to his parent's proposal. This shows her good nature.

Seth has introduced many women characters in his novel and it shows how much concern and respect he has given towards women. So, women of strong, women of conformity and women of conviction are portrayed as having their own qualities. All these characters are needed to this male dominant society to keep peace of mind and unity in the family and the society.

Women are created as very strong and sensitive, lovable and responsible, confident and determined as they realize their potential and the special power within themselves. All these women must understand and be aware of their original beauty within themselves than the outer beauty.

References

1. Anand, Mulk Raj, *Untouchable,* New Delhi: Arnold Publishers, 1981.
2. Agarwalla and *S.S. Vikram Seth's A Suitable Boy: Search for an Indian Identity,* New Delhi: Prestige, 1995.
3. Asani and M. Shyam, *Critical Response to Indian English Fiction,* Delhi, 1985.
4. Desai and Anita *Cry, The Peacock.* Delhi: Orient Paperbacks, 1980.
5. Deshpande and Shasi, *That Long Silence,* New Delhi: Penguin Books, 1989.
6. Devanesen and Mithran, "A Note on the play", *Dance Like a Man* in *Collected Plays* Mahesh Dattani, New Delhi: Penguin Books, 2000.
7. R.K. Dhawan and Tanu Pant, *The plays of Mahesh Dattani: A Critical Response,* New Delhi, Penguin India, 2000.
8. Jain, Jasbir, *Anita Desai: Indian English Novelists,* ed. Madhusudhanan Prasad. New Delhi: Sterling, 1982.
9. Kuthari Chaudhuri and Asha, *Contemporary Indian Writers in English Mahesh Dattani,* New Delhi: Foundation Books Pvt. Ltd, Cambridge House, 2005.
10. I.D. Pandian, *Arundhati Roy: Life and Work,* Bhaskar Publication, 2009.
11. F.M. Patlel, *Feminism in contemporary Indian women writers,* Aavishkar Publishers Distributors, Jaipur 30, 2003.
12. B. Rao and Ramachandra, *The Novels of Anita Desai,* New Delhi: Kalyani, 1977.
13. Roy and Arundhati, *The God of Small Things,* India Ink, 1997.

14. Sharma Siddhartha, *Shashi Deshpande's Novel's A feminist study* Atlantic Publishers &Distributors (p) Ltd., Pp.100, 2011.
15. R.S. Sharma, *Anita Desai,* New Delhi: Arnold-Heineann, 1981.
16. Sree S. Prasanna, *Woman in the novels of Shasi Deshpande: A study* published by Prabhat.
17. B.L. Tripathi, *Anita Desai: Dimensions of the Inner World*, New Delhi, Prestige.